SINCE
SINAI

A Convert's Path to Judaism

SHANNON GONYOU

For information, contact
MSI Press LLC
1760-F Airline Hwy, #203
Hollister, CA 95023

Cover Artist:
Cover design: Opeyemi Ikuborije
Layout & typesetting: Opeyemi Ikuborije
Copyediting: Betty Lou Leaver
Editing: Marie Valentine

Library of Congress Control Number: 2021925202
ISBN: 978-1-957354-00-2

CONTENTS

I've never written a book before, and I'm a little overwhelmed by the heaviness of my first book being about something so deeply personal, historically rich, and philosophically complex. Religion can be difficult to talk about. For that reason, in everyday life, I mostly don't. Many of my acquaintances know that I converted to Judaism, but I sense that they're afraid to ask why. This isn't necessarily a bad thing because while I love to talk about Judaism, I don't love that people often expect me to opine on the correctness of my belief system in comparison to theirs. Because of that, it feels important to preface this one-way conversation with a note about what my book is not equipped to do.

This book cannot definitively help you decide whether you should become Jewish. It cannot meaningfully help you decide whether conversion is ultimately right for you, nor which movement of Judaism to choose. This book will not purport to tell you which religion is right or wrong because I don't think spirituality is a matter of fact versus fiction as much as it's a matter of feeling at home in your own belief system. This book is certainly not meant to convince anyone to leave Catholicism or Christianity like I did. If you're happy with your spiritual beliefs—or lack of spiritual beliefs—I am very happy for you.

This book cannot serve as a scholarly guide to Jewish versus Christian theology. I only feel qualified to speak on my *experiences* with religion, not to be the definitive voice on what each faith stands for. Other Christians experience Christianity differently than I did, and other Jews experience Judaism differently. I also don't want anyone to think that all Jewish converts were formerly Christian. Some are, many are not. If you are reading this book to find out what conversion programs are like and you don't harbor any curiosity about what led me from Catholicism to Judaism, you are more than welcome to skip to Chapter 9. I'll never know!

This book isn't meant to be an accounting of what Jews believe. Other authors have covered that topic extensively, and different Jews believe different things; that's half the fun. I'm not going to tell you what I think happens after we die, nor will I be using this book to share my thoughts on the State of Israel. This book also cannot convince anybody that following any religion is inherently good. Maybe a religious institution harmed you, or maybe you're a very comfortable atheist who doesn't get the draw of organized religion. You have my respect, anyway.

What this book *can* do is tell the story of one convert (me) in order to (hopefully) de-mystify the process of why someone who grew up without knowing more than three Jews would want to later become Jewish herself. In the name of transparency, I grew up Roman Catholic and was involved in churches of various denominations for 25 years of my life. I later converted under the auspices of the Conservative Judaism movement in the United States, often called Masorti Judaism outside of North America. I am not in a position to speak to the ways in which Orthodox, Reform, Reconstructionist, or other conversion processes differ, and this book will not disparage any of those movements. In fact, now that I live in New York

City, I attend events hosted by many denominations, from Chabad to post-denominational.

You might be curious about what it is that I believe. I'm not presenting any of my ideas as "Truth," but everyone has a bias. It's important to know mine up front. I am a Jew who identifies with the American Conservative movement. I believe, as my wise cantor Liz Berke once suggested, in "one God or less." I do not believe that God is a man or my father. I read the Torah as rich and timeless literature with many possible meanings for our lives today. I believe that our matriarchs and patriarchs did some things well and also made mistakes, much like us. I believe that community traditions often have value even in the absence of an explanation. I believe that you've found your religious sweet spot when you feel both empowered and challenged by your practice.

I am a fervent believer that the faithful are called to take care of the earth and to take care of each other. I believe that every person you meet was created *b'tzelem Elohim*, or in the image of the divine. Because of that, I believe in working to create a Jewish community that supports women, Jews of color, queer and trans Jews, patrilineal Jews, interfaith families, and converts. I think that sex-positivity is a better framework for young adults than "purity," but if you disagree, definitely skip Chapter 3. I believe that we should strive to treat the dead with respect and mourners with great care and that helping mourners cope and move on after a loss is an essential function of the community. I believe that to sin, per the Hebrew definition, simply means to "miss the mark." I believe that humans are not inherently sinners and do not need to be saved from our sinfulness; we just need to be surrounded by people who can help us grow as we muck our way through life. I love the process of *tshuva*, the Jewish version of making amends. I believe that we are all God's partners in creation, and that means that we should be careful and intentional about the things we do and say. I think that living a life of morality and service is important, whether you're conventionally religious or not. I believe that no one can tell anyone else what the right decisions for themselves are, but our religious communities can provide a helpful framework for working through life's more trying moments. I believe that changing one's mind is a sign of strength, not flimsiness. I believe that forgiveness is generally good but is not always required. I believe that we have so much to work on in this life that time spent thinking about a hypothetical next life is not usually time well spent. I believe that Jesus was a controversial member of the Jewish community and not that he was a deity. Finally, I believe the best thing about Judaism is that other Jews can disagree on most of this and we'll probably still be able to share a Shabbat dinner in peace.

ACKNOWLEDGEMENTS

This book would not have happened without Rabbi Rubenstein in a number of ways. Most obviously, he oversaw my conversion, without which this book would have been rendered moot. But more important, he read, edited, and asked questions about every chapter of this book to ensure its clarity and accuracy from a Jewish standpoint. He was a constant cheerleader for this book and continues to be a big supporter of our family and our Jewish journey.

Everyone asked how I found time to write while also working a full-time job and parenting. Mostly, the key was that my husband did the things I didn't have time for: dishes, baby gymnastics class, changing the rabbit's litter box, brewing pots of tea. Without him stepping up around the house—and giving up some of the little social time we have with one another in the evenings—this book would have remained permanently unwritten. Travis has said "yes" a lot, from the day that I asked him to join the Jews by Choice program to the day that I signed a publishing contract. I can never express enough gratitude.

There were also people who spot-checked my memory and helped me reconstruct things that had transpired years ago. Thank you to Amelia Parnis, Yesenia Grijalva, Chris Mann, Stephanie Berliant, and Liz Berke, all of whom provided invaluable comments during the editing process. I also pestered my author friends Raechel Tiffe and Jillian Keenan with questions about the publishing process. They were open and informative. It takes a village to write a memoir, and my village was extremely helpful.

Finally, thanks to Betty Lou Leaver and her team at MSI Press for taking a chance on my little project and my amazing publicist Jessie Glenn for bringing unparalleled enthusiasm to the table. I learned quickly that selling a book is harder than writing a book, so I consider myself lucky to have found experts in the field who are both honest and kind.

B"H and BS"D.

CHAPTER 1

"Life is a matter of choices, and every choice you make makes you." —*John C. Maxwell*

I told my husband that I wanted to convert to Judaism on Christmas Eve. We were sitting in our Chevy Impala in a grocery store parking lot in Ann Arbor, Michigan when I broached the topic. We were living in Chicago at the time, but we had traveled back to Michigan for the holidays. Christmas gifts for our family members were toppling over in the back seat, and a tin box of snowman-shaped Christmas cookies from my mother-in-law rested heavily on my lap. We had just picked up some ingredient that my mom had forgotten to buy for Christmas Eve dinner, and we were supposed to be making a quick trip back to our hotel room to change clothes before heading to the celebration. I decided that during this quick ten-minute jaunt from a grocery store to the Extended Stay Briarwood Mall, on the precipice of our family Christmas celebration, that I would casually throw out the idea of becoming Jewish.

I admit that the timing was bad. As we navigated our way through the darkened parking lot, snowflakes dancing above us, Travis adjusted the radio dial, and the sound of "The First Noel" filled the car—not a great background track for the conversation we were about to have. Travis glanced side to side and made a left-hand turn onto the empty road. The drive was short, so I needed to speak quickly. I sat up straight and cleared my throat.

"After this trip," I began, "I'd like to take a class back in Chicago. It starts in early January."

"What kind of class?" Travis asked, already skeptical.

"I found a class near us about Judaism," I told him tentatively. "I've been curious about Judaism for a long time, and I'd really like to go. I can go by myself, but I thought it would be nice if we could explore it together—if you have time and all." I looked down at my hands and held my breath.

"Okay," he replied, running a gloved hand along the steering wheel, "I would be interested in learning about Judaism. Our schedules are a little tight right now, though. Maybe we can find a different time to take the class."

"It's not so much a class," I said, choosing my words carefully. "It is a class, but it's also more of a program for people who want to convert to Judaism."

"We're not converting to Judaism." He looked confused more than troubled.

"Well … we *could*." I pointed out innocently, "If we take the class."

"Shannon!" Travis exclaimed, "We are not converting to Judaism. Please tell me we're not converting to Judaism." I let the silence speak for itself. I had no intention of forcing Travis to convert, but my own mind was basically made up at this point.

"Oh, my God!" was all he said.

"I think the Jews refer to God as *Hashem*," I joked lightly.

"Shannon..." he repeated, already exhausted with the conversation. We had arrived back at the hotel, and I hadn't made much ground. Travis put the car in park, and we stared at each other. The silence was thick and uncomfortable.

I understood his hesitation. The year had been long for both of us. The prior December, we had married and, two weeks later, had celebrated my law school graduation. After enjoying a long honeymoon, we moved into a new apartment in Chicago, and our married life took off at a sprint. I studied for the Illinois Bar Exam while coaching gymnastics at a local gym to earn spare income. After the Bar, I started a fellowship at the Cook County Public Guardian's Office while still coaching on evenings and weekends.

Also in law school, Travis had spent every weekend during the summer driving back and forth from his summer job in Detroit to our apartment in Chicago. In the fall, my fellowship ended, and I started a career in the litigation department of a large law firm, notorious for being demanding and high-pressure.

Travis continued on to his last year of law school. We tried to keep up with a number of hobbies, from competitive fencing to learning Italian. We both got up early every day to hit the gym and stayed up late to work and study. We were also practicing Catholics. Obligations and activities filled our lives to bursting. So why, I'm sure Travis was wondering, would I complicate the life we had created by suggesting that we become Jewish? That question—why would I decide to become Jewish—is this book's *raison d'être*.

"We could wait," I conceded. "I know the timing feels awful. I know how busy we are. Yet, I can't stop thinking about it, and you know how I get when an idea takes hold. I've held my tongue for as long as possible. I don't want to throw our lives into upheaval. I wouldn't be saying anything if it weren't burning me up inside."

"It's Christmas Eve!" Travis sighed. "And converting from Catholicism to Judaism is most certainly an upheaval. What made you even think of this?"

"Well ..." I glanced at our digital clock, its red numbers glowing aggressively. I didn't have much time to explain. We would be late to dinner. And in any case, it seemed impossible to explain.

A month prior to this poorly executed car ambush, I had stumbled across a "Jews by Choice" conversion program at Anshe Emet, a Conservative synagogue less than a mile from our apartment in Chicago.

"Stumbled" might be a disingenuous term. It was no accident that I was spending my limited spare time Googling "how to convert to Judaism?" or "how to know if you should be Jewish?" or "are converts accepted as Jews?" I'm pretty sure that the course came up when I Googled some variation of "become a Jew in Chicago." You can truly find anything on the internet.

Apparently, Chicago had so many aspiring Jewish converts that classes were offered at multiple synagogues in the city and suburbs. Given this much interest, maybe the idea of converting wasn't so far-fetched, after all. I downloaded the course schedule for Anshe Emet's program, the closest one to where we lived in the city. The program was divided into fall and winter semesters, making January an ideal time to start—the short answer to why we were discussing a major religious identity shift on a Christian holiday.

"I get that you want to take the class," Travis said when I told him about my incessant Googling, "But I still don't know why we have to become Jewish. Isn't it enough to learn about Judaism?"

"I don't think it will be enough for me to learn from a distance," I explained.

"Why?" he asked. He had to turn down the Christmas music in order to focus on what I was saying. It is hard to make a case for Judaism with "Frosty the Snowman" playing in the background, so I appreciated that.

"I don't feel at home in Catholicism," I said, "I'm increasingly uneasy about trying to make a home for our future children there. I have doubts about Jesus dying on the cross to save us because I don't think we needed to be saved, at least not in the way that Christianity teaches. I admire Jesus' teachings, but I'm growing uncomfortable with the human sacrifice narrative."

"Those are significant developments," he admitted uneasily.

"I don't see the merits of using a priest as a sort of conduit between God and myself," I continued. "The Christian concept of the afterlife doesn't comfort me like it should. And I don't feel anything when I take communion. I'm acting out the role of a Catholic, but I'm not feeling what I want to feel in my spiritual life."

It felt like Catholicism had been arbitrarily assigned to me when I was born into a Catholic family and baptized before I could hold my own head up. Of the many places to find a connection to spirituality, Judaism was the one that consistently tugged at me. I insisted that if spirituality were an open field, Catholicism would reflect being forced to sit on the outskirts of the field in an uncomfortable lawn chair. I reminded Travis that the last time that we had attended a charismatic Catholic Church in search of a more upbeat service, the priest spent half an hour railing against gay marriage while Travis balled up his fists and turned red in the face. I appreciated that the Church was generally open to doubters and questioners, but it had moved beyond friendly disagreement. I had to leave, and I was going to leave for Judaism.

"Plus, honestly," I finished, "I have no idea what you believe about God or Jesus or saints or the Bible. We go to Mass and talk about being good people, but though we have been together for years, I have no idea what you actually think about Church doctrine. That makes me feel like maybe we're in this thing for the wrong reasons. Out of habit or something. I don't know. I don't want to speak for you, but maybe you have doubts, too." I gave Travis some time to digest everything I had said.

I could tell that he was grinding his teeth. He looked tired.

"I don't disagree," he said finally, "But I don't know if I'm ready to confront that by becoming Jewish right now."

This was more headway than I thought I'd make. It sounded like his objections were based on how difficult the journey to conversion would be rather than his attachment to Christian theology. That gave me some hope that we might be able to make this a family project.

"Like I said, I keep going back to the Jews by Choice program webpage and scrolling through it longingly," I explained sheepishly. "There will never be a good time for this type of undertaking. There will always be work, travel, kids, or another barrier in the way. There is no time like the present, as they say."

"I'm worried that we won't fit in," he said finally.

"I think it's bound to feel like that for the first generation of converts," I countered. "Our child won't have to be a convert, though. Our child can be raised Jewish. Our great-great-grandchildren might not even remember that we converted."

"I'm not worried about our great-great-grandchildren," he said dismissively. "But I do want to pick the right religion for our children."

I could see the gears turning now. Kids weren't a theoretical future construct to us. Travis and I were actively trying to get pregnant. I had stocked up on prenatal vitamins and found an app to track my ovulation. I was nothing if not organized about the endeavor. We both desperately wanted to avoid bringing a child into a religion not right for our family.

"Judaism can be our family's religion," I said, "Something that we can learn and pass down. It will be hard in the beginning, but we can do it."

"It's a beautiful religion, and I have a lot of respect for it," Travis said thoughtfully, "But Jews have their own history as a people. It's more than a religion. I have never met someone who woke up and decided to become Jewish."

"What about Cindy on *Orange is the New Black*?" I asked.

"Really?" he asked incredulously.

"Yes!" I exclaimed. "Cindy only had one rabbi on her *beit din* instead of three. She immersed herself in a lake with no rabbinical supervision, but you had to have gotten the point." (A *beit din* is a religious court, and most, but not all, denominations of Judaism require a court of three rabbis to approve a conversion. Cindy's conversion was unconventional but memorable as far as pop-culture references go.)

"I don't know any *real* people who have converted," he clarified, not feeling swayed by my Netflix reference.

"We can do it," I repeated. "I've read all about it. You convert to Judaism by studying for a long time under the guidance of a rabbi, and then you sit for a *beit din* where three rabbis engage you in conversation about the sincerity of your conversion. Then you pick a Hebrew name, immerse yourself thrice in some water, and you emerge as Jewish as Abraham and Sarah themselves."

"Fine. We could do it. But why?" For Travis, the *why* was just as pressing as the *how*.

It surprises no one that I am constantly asked *why* I converted. Why did you convert to Judaism, an ancient non-evangelizing tradition often known for questioning the sincerity of converts long after the conversion process is complete? Why did you join a perpetually persecuted branch of the Abrahamic religions when that religion did absolutely nothing to seek you out? Why did you throw away your chance to be in the national and global majority solely because the Jesus story doesn't add up for you? I understand the urge to question converts. I do. But the answers to these questions are extremely personal and not prone to quick response. I usually end up mumbling something about "just wanting to" and changing the topic.

In my eyes, the lucky Jews convert for marriage. It's a perfectly sensible excuse to become a Jew without anyone batting an eye. Telling someone that you converted for a spouse in the name of family unity is not particularly remarkable. It's a neat and simple explanation. In fact, I sometimes lie and tell strangers or co-workers that I converted for marriage when they ask. It's not because I'm a serial fibber but because having to repeatedly re-hash a major life decision is far more emotionally exhausting than saying yes when asked if I converted for my husband.

Other Jews convert because they take a DNA test that indicates they may have Ashkenazi or Sephardi ancestry. Excited about this newfound revelation, the previously non-Jewish person starts to study the Jewish faith and decides to convert formally. Unfortunately, 23&Me awarded me less than 1% Jewish ancestry and promptly deleted it months later when the system ascertained that I was more likely Iberian. Wonderful. Travis's family was Italian Catholic and French Catholic as far back as the family tree would go.

Simply: I converted only because I wanted to. There are a number of good explanations for why I might want to be Jewish. The most obvious is that the Jewish teachings struck me as good and true. Not true in the sense that I think Noah's Ark really sailed the seas thousands of years ago but true in the sense that they carry a lot of practical wisdom for day-to-day living in the modern world. Life presents us with challenges and questions, and Judaism provides answers and guidance that resonate with the wisest and most discerning part of my soul. But acknowledging that Jewish teachings are wise is probably not enough on its own to inspire people to undergo the rigorous process of converting. I longed to offer Travis— and everyone else for that matter—a digestible justification for my choice to convert.

Immediately after law school, I took part in a Holocaust studies trip to Germany and Poland with FASPE, or Fellowships at Auschwitz for the Study of

Professional Ethics. Through the program, I spent time studying Jewish history in Berlin and walking reverently through Auschwitz in Poland. Being at Auschwitz changed me, that much I'm sure of. Learning about the history of Judaism before, during, and after World War II was a moving experience. However, as much of an impact that the trip had, it wasn't the one thing that made me want to become Jewish. In fact, it made me wonder if the realities of Jewish history would make it impossible to fit in as a brand-new member of the community.

I joined a sorority as an undergraduate student at the University of Michigan. Jewish students were heavily represented in the Greek Life population and in the campus population at large. I met a lot of Jewish students during college, many of whom I consider close friends. But aside from knowing that they were Jewish and that some of them didn't eat pork, I wasn't clear on what their Jewish practice actually entailed. My first time really encountering a Jewish practice was at my friend Leah's home during the summer break before my sophomore year. I spent a beautiful Shabbat evening in Needham, Massachusetts with Leah and her high school friends. I was touched by the idea of setting aside time for family on the Sabbath; of enjoying fresh fruit and friendly conversation by candlelight. When I put a quarter in the Steinberg's *tzedakah* box—a small box kept in Jewish homes to collect money for charity—I felt like family. Some of Leah's friends didn't drive on the Sabbath. They each seemed to observe varying levels of *kashrut* (in English, kosher). But the community feel wasn't diminished in the slightest by variations in practice. I was really touched.

As beautiful as that visit was, it wasn't the one thing that made me want to be Jewish.

My favorite professor in law school happened to be an Orthodox Jew. She was a gentle but fiercely brilliant woman who devoted her career to helping struggling families in Michigan access safe housing and adequate medical care for their children. She was a committed feminist and a damn good lawyer. I knew she kept a kosher home and was religious. I was intrigued by her faith, but I never directly asked her about it. I had plenty of smart, inspiring professors who were Jewish, but I did not need to convert in order to admire them.

I can't even say that a beautiful Jewish funeral or wedding inspired me, because I'd never been to any of those celebrations at the time of my conversion. (At least not a real one. Our conversion course involved a very educational *bris* of a stuffed animal). I heard about my friends' bar mitzvah and bat mitzvah celebrations, but no one in my hometown had celebrated one. No one had ever invited me to a Jewish summer camp or even an interfaith wedding.

It would be accurate to say that a combination of these experiences added up to the idea that I should convert. It's hard to say. In truth, I wanted to be Jewish because the idea came to me and refused to leave. Every time I tried to add more color to the explanation than that, I gave a markedly different answer than the last time I'd answered the question.

When I met with the kind, soft-spoken cantor who ran the local conversion course, I told her that I wanted to be Jewish because it was, to me, a more breathable form of monotheism. And that reason was true. Spiritual, but not necessarily rigid; reverent, but not without humor; intellectual, but not without meaning. I told my friend Alana that the Jewish community was small but remarkably cohesive and that I felt inexplicably drawn to their peoplehood. That was also true. I told my *beit din*, the three rabbis who oversaw my conversion, that I wanted to be Jewish because the rituals of Jewish life and the rhythm of the Hebrew calendar helped me turn the mundane into something reflective and powerful. And that was definitely true. Those are all good reasons, and they are all true. But none of them are the *sole* reason that I became Jewish.

My last-ditch effort is to blame it on divine intervention, destiny, whatever you want to call it. There is an idea in Judaism that converts' souls were at Sinai with our Jewish ancestors. Our souls were destined for the Torah. So, even though we aren't born into Jewish families, our souls find their way back to the community through conversion. It has remained the explanation that comes closest to getting at the truth about Jewish conversion from my perspective: the decision to convert is born in one's heart and soul rather than one's head. Conversion feels like an innate idea that, once awakened, refuses to go away. That you should become Jewish starts to feel as obvious as the fact you love your favorite food or feel attracted to your partner(s). Most early converts don't stop thinking about conversion until they finally work up the courage to email a rabbi and begin the process in earnest. The idea was there all along; I just needed to identify it and act on it at the right time. Or, of course, conversion might not enter your mind until your spouse slaps you in the face with the idea of becoming Jewish on the eve of your favorite Christian holiday.

In the safe cocoon of our Impala, I was still making my case to Travis.

"I've tried other churches," I told him, "You know I have. I feel like Judaism is my home, and I can't make myself stop thinking that."

"We went to Mass a week ago!" Travis sighed. "And now you'd like to stop going?"

"Well, yeah," I explained, "We have to not be Catholic in order to be Jewish, but otherwise, the good news is that there aren't many 'rules' about how to be Jewish. That's the whole draw."

"I don't know if I believe what Jews believe. I don't know what Jews believe."

"Do you believe that Jesus is the son of God who died on a cross to absolve mankind of sin?" I asked back.

"I don't know," he said.

"Our priests would be disheartened to hear that," I replied. "It sounds like we need to start from scratch and figure it out."

"Theology aside, the Jewish people suffered a Holocaust," he explained, as if I hadn't been standing in the ruins of Auschwitz during my FASPE fellowship program. "They suffered centuries of persecution before that. It's more than a belief system. It's a culture and a history."

"Half of the conversion courses are spent addressing that," I assured him.

"What will people think of us? Of me? They're going to think we're flakey or disingenuous."

"There's nothing more disingenuous than going to Mass every week when you no longer believe," I told him.

An uneasy silence returned. I focused on the soft hum of our car's heating system and the snowflakes dancing around outside of the windshield. Travis chewed his lip anxiously. The car's digital clock showed that three minutes had passed since either of us had last spoken. Three became five. Five became seven. Snowflakes continued to fall and dissolve against our windshield.

I knew that I needed to say *something*, but it's understandably hard to explain that you wish to overhaul your entire religious belief system in ten minutes or less. I ran my finger across the cartoon snowman on my cookie tin.

"I already emailed the nice lady who runs the Jews by Choice program in Chicago," I finally said with an apologetic shrug, "So, I'm going to go check it out. You don't have to come with me, but I think it will be pretty low pressure either way. The Jews aren't known to evangelize."

Travis sighed the sigh of a man who knew that his wife's mind had been made up. His hand hovered over the radio dial. He was undoubtedly contemplating whether this was a bad time to turn the Christmas music back on.

"We can go to the class to explore the idea," he said finally. "I'm not committing to actually doing the conversion."

"Of course," I said, unceremoniously dumping the Christmas cookie tin off of my lap. "You absolutely don't have to. It doesn't have to be something we do as a family. I need to do it for myself."

"I love Christmas," Travis grumbled pathetically.

"I don't think the rabbis are going to pry the Starbucks eggnog latte out of your hypothetically Jewish hands," I promised. "Please give it a chance."

"We'll give it a chance," he confirmed as we climbed out of the car. "But I want you to know that Christmas brings me a lot of joy. It's my favorite time of year."

"So you've said," I smirked, looping my arm through his and pulling him toward the hotel lobby.

With my secret out in the open, I felt that I could enjoy Christmas Eve, even if it was going to be my last as a non-Jew.

CHAPTER 2

"Life is like riding a bicycle. To keep your
balance, you must keep moving."
—*Albert Einstein*

My mom took the news that I wanted to become
Jewish about as well as Travis did. I waited until I was
four months into the conversion program so that I could
ensure that things were moving in the right direction
before I alarmed her with the news. I needed to be in
New York City for a FASPE program reunion, so I invited
my mom to come along and sightsee between program
sessions. She had never been to the city before. What
better place to broach the subject, I had thought, than a
city with such a large concentration of Jews?

If you are imagining that I carefully planned this
conversation based on what I had learned from winging
it with Travis, you are wrong. I'm not a girl who learns
lessons that easily.

With only a very vague outline of what I needed to
say in my head, I dragged my mom from our Airbnb on
the Upper West Side to Junior's Bakery in Times Square.

At the time, I was seven weeks pregnant and constantly on the verge of vomiting. I ordered myself a decaf latte and a black-and-white cookie, which I picked at halfheartedly to keep the nausea at bay. As we ate, my mom asked me questions about my pregnancy and about the itinerary for our trip. She wanted to see a show on Broadway.

A good segue has never been my forte, so I promised her that we would snag last-minute tickets for a show and promptly decided that this would be a perfect time to bring up the fact that I was abandoning our lifelong shared religious faith. I cleared my throat and set down my mug with a clink.

My mom could sense a storm brewing. She had been here before. My mother loves me, but she does not always understand my choices. She waited patiently for what was to come.

"Would you be offended if I switched my religion a bit? We were thinking of converting to Judaism." I used the phrase "a bit" as if converting from Roman Catholicism to Judaism was a little technicality, akin to leaving a Presbyterian church to become Methodist.

"You're already Catholic," my mom said flatly, as if I was suggesting that I should purchase a new iPhone when I already had a perfectly good one in my hand.

"I recall," I said uncomfortably. "I was raised Catholic, yes. And it's a wonderful religion in a lot of ways. But it doesn't feel like the right religion for me and my growing family, so I was thinking about becoming Jewish."

I put my hands over my stomach where my blueberry-sized daughter was growing. Why didn't I want to raise her Catholic? The fact that women can't aspire to the same leadership positions as men was one reason. I had no desire to be a priest, but the lack of female leadership created a problem for me. It vexed me that Church doctrine was often entangled with American political positions. Sometimes, attending a Catholic event felt like attending the Republican National Convention. I was bothered by the fact that an increasing number of Churches were purporting to fully support and welcome the LGBTQ community while refusing to open the sacrament of matrimony to those same people. As an adoptee, I was a little bothered by the way that my pregnant birth mother had practically been shunned for her unplanned pregnancy 25 years prior. And, of course, increasingly thorny sex abuse scandals within the Catholic Church were coming to light while I was finishing law school.

I think my mother would have been sympathetic to any of these things, but more than likely she'd wave her hand and encourage me to join the Lutherans instead. There are plenty of Christian denominations to choose from, and certainly some movement could have solved nearly all of my issues. But that's not what I wanted to do. Beyond that, if I made a fuss about why I was leaving, my mom might feel like raising me Catholic was a mistake. I didn't see it that way. Catholicism was the best thing she knew, and there were many things that made it a beautiful tradition. It wasn't anyone's fault that another tradition had captured my heart. I wanted to look forward at all of the things that would be great about being Jewish rather than looking back and dissecting why Christianity had fallen flat for me in the end.

"Judaism feels better for our family," I tried.

"I didn't realize you could become Jewish. Don't you have to be born Jewish?" my mom asked. This is a common misconception. You can wake up one day and decide to give your life to Jesus, sure, but the idea that someone would wake up and decide to become Jewish gives people a lot of heartburn.

"It's a religion," I explained. "The ethnic component is really complicated. Actually, according to a Pew study, one in six American Jews are actually converts. Do you remember Ruth? From the Bible? She converted. Judaism is full of converts. I'll be in good company."

"No, I don't remember Ruth," my mom sighed. "And a Pew study, seriously?" My mom took a bite of her side of the black-and-white cookie.

"There was nothing wrong with growing up Catholic," I assured her. "It's not the best fit anymore, and that is okay."

"You like being Catholic," my mom countered.

I smiled weakly. I realized that I shouldn't have kicked off the conversation by asking whether conversion would offend my mom. My conversion wasn't about my mother's feelings, or anyone else's feelings for that matter. It wasn't going to be open to negotiation. I needed to shift gears.

"I thought maybe we could go to a synagogue for Shabbat services tonight. There's one nearby called Town and Village," I suggested. "It's a Friday, and the evening service is really lovely. You can check it out and get to know the community a little bit." (It is a funny twist of fate that when we eventually moved to New York City, Town and Village was the Conservative synagogue closest to our apartment and the one where we became members).

"No," said my mom without looking up from the cookie. "Absolutely not."

"Okay," I nodded. "What about a Jewish museum?"

"I want to go to a Broadway show," my mom repeated. She would need more time to digest this news.

"Hey, by the way, who are this baby's godparents going to be?" my mom asked, innocently taking a gulp of her iced tea. I was confused by the question. I squinted at her and waited for her to say that she was joking, but she didn't. Perhaps she didn't quite understand the conversion situation.

"The baby won't be baptized," I explained, "So, we won't need godparents."

"What do you mean, the baby won't be baptized?" my mom asked, staring blankly. I looked around to make sure that no one was eavesdropping. I regretted not telling her the conversion news at our Airbnb.

"I'm not out of the first trimester yet," I responded quietly. "Let's revisit this all later." I could tell that if my mom was still talking about baptism, we weren't exactly on the same page about the conversion.

"Which show are we going to get tickets to?" my mom asked.

We didn't discuss my conversion for the rest of the trip. In fact, we didn't exactly discuss it again until my daughter's baby naming almost a full year later. We still rarely discuss it. One of the hardest aspects of conversion is that your family doesn't convert with you. Family members might want neat and tidy explanations for the conversion that don't reflect the complexity of the decision. I had to lower my expectations and accept that people might never understand the choice, but they could come to respect it.

I don't think my mom had ever met a Jew other than our family physician, so it's unsurprising that she wouldn't know anything about Judaism. In fact, I didn't know anything about Judaism before college. On the other hand, my family had never been Catholicism's biggest cheerleaders, either.

I grew up in a blue-collar suburb of Detroit. When I was born in 1992, the population was well over 90% white, and according to the most recent census I can find online, the city was 0.0 percent Jewish. My dad was Catholic. My mom was Protestant. Almost everyone that I knew was formally Catholic even if their families rarely went to Mass. If they weren't Catholic, they were Baptist or some other Christian denomination. Since it was the '90s, public schools were still in the habit of putting up Christmas and Easter decorations. I assumed that everyone was Christian unless they told me otherwise, and for years, no one ever did.

Like any Christian kid, I looked forward to holidays. I understood that Christmas and Easter were holy because they celebrated the birth and death of Jesus, but holidays were marked by the non-religious traditions of family meals, presents, decorations, and time off from school. On Christmas Eve, we would drive the three blocks from our house to my aunt's house to spend the evening with my father's side of the family. Since I didn't have any siblings, my two older cousins, Matthew and Corey, functioned as my brothers. They were both more than five years my senior and I was fascinated by everything they did. They made me laugh, taught me to swear, and let me watch while they played table tennis and poker. Our mothers would make pierogis from scratch and we would devour them with ladles of fresh, melted butter.

On Christmas morning, I would wake my parents up before sunrise and tear through all of my gifts from Santa. Santa conveniently brought me all of the annoying gifts that my mother swore she would never buy for me, like giant beanbag chairs and Pokémon video games. I loved giving my parents gifts, too. It was always total junk, like poorly constructed bird houses and neon orange screwdrivers, but surprising people with tokens of my affection has remained one of my favorite things to do well into adulthood.

Once the wrapping paper had been cleaned up, we drove three blocks in the opposite direction of my aunt's house to visit my grandmother. My mother's side of the family included all of my younger cousins from out of state, whom I adored feeding and dressing up and horsing around with.

Every one of the six kids on my mom's side of the family was adopted, but on Christmas, the beauty of our patchwork family was evident. I would teach my younger cousins how to do forward rolls and cartwheels, or we would all go outside and climb my grandmother's tree while she shook her head disapprovingly from the doorway.

My grandma's house featured a freshly cut Christmas tree with twinkling rainbow-colored lights. The whole house smelled like pine. My mom and aunts would spend the afternoon making deviled eggs, Jell-O salad, and a huge honey-baked ham. Not once did we go to Church on Christmas, and we didn't go on Easter, either. My parents blamed it on the crowds, but they didn't jump to attend Mass any other day of the year either. The name Jesus never came up around the holidays.

Later, the prospect of conversion would be less daunting knowing that my parents would be flustered by my refusal to eat Christmas ham, but they wouldn't be kept up at night with thoughts of me burning in hell for eternity. Becoming Jewish would make me different from my family in some ways, but holidays were really about being together more than they were about our shared belief in Christianity. In other words, my parents would have preferred me to stay culturally Christian but are neutral on whether I'm religiously Christian. Deeply religious Christian families compound the challenges for converts. Different challenges undoubtedly exist for converts raised in anti-theist homes. Watching people change is hard. Loving people means letting them change anyway.

As for going to Mass on non-holidays, at the time that I came into the world, my mom and dad were not really churchgoing people. The priest who was meant to baptize me agreed to do so only under the condition that they continue to bring me to church. I'm not clear on why it was so important to them to have me baptized in the first place. Perhaps because he grew up going to Catholic school my dad felt pressure to pass on the faith despite his admittedly terrible experience with Catholic schooling. Maybe because my birth mother had requested that my parents raise me Catholic after my adoption they felt pressure to fulfill the promise even if they weren't staunch believers. Maybe, on some level, they really did think that I would be doomed to the fires of hell without a baptism ceremony. A lifetime of participating in services that they didn't care about apparently seemed like a fair trade for what could be eternal salvation for me. The deal having been concluded, my parents made good on their promise by dragging me—often complaining—to St. Thomas the Apostle Catholic Church on one Sunday each month. Getting to church involved a somewhat long, scenic drive from our home in the suburbs to our church on the outskirts of Detroit. When I realized that there were plenty of churches closer to home, I asked my parents what the deal was.

"We don't like any of those priests," my mom explained vaguely.

What my parents saw in this particular priest, I'll never know. In my mind, Mass was boring, and sitting still for sixty minutes was torture. I spent most of my time in church digging my fingernail into the softened wood of the back pews or counting the diagonal wooden rafters against the high, bright white ceiling. I would sneak into the hallway and listen to the hum and splash of the drinking fountain, scuffing my nice church shoes against the dirty, cracked beige tiles. I would grab onto a flimsy paper plate on those coveted "donut Sundays" and savor the feeling of a glazed donut dissolving on my tongue, its saccharine sweetness a sharp contrast to the bite of communion wine. I grew familiar with the prayers that were recited every week at Mass but mostly as a way to gauge how close to the end of the service we were. The church was my playground more than it was my sanctuary. When I was too old to run around and hide under the back pew with the other youngsters of the community, I took to pulling on my dad's shirt sleeve and asking him when we could go home.

"How many more minutes until it's over? How many more seconds?" I would beg.

"One hundred thousand eighty-five seconds," my dad would whisper back. It was always a made-up number, and it always sounded like too much.

After approximately 60 minutes, 19 trips to the drinking fountain, one Our Father, and seven or so friendly "peace be with you" handshakes, we would head back to the parking lot where I would promptly pray that my parents would forget to bring me next month. If you would have told me that I would one day happily sit through Shabbat services that exceed 2 hours in length and Yom Kippur services that essentially last all day, young Shannon would have fainted from the shock of it.

Instead of forgetting about the whole church thing, my parents upped the ante by signing me up for catechism classes, which were required for all children who hoped to participate in the First Communion ceremony. I was desperate to participate in First Communion, not for any spiritual reason but because it was the only way to get my grimy 7-year-old hands on a communion wafer, which had been denied to me every other week of my pained young existence. Jealousy is a heck of a drug, as they say. My mom was very enthusiastic about picking out a First Communion gown, and my parents even threw me a backyard barbeque with close family and friends to celebrate. This was in spite of the fact that my mom never became Catholic and sat out the Eucharist portion of Mass every time we went.

Anyone who knew me as a child would say that I was a model student. Truly. I was an overachiever, so much so that I wept for an entire recess period when I spelled a bonus word wrong on a second-grade spelling test. I wrote my teacher an impassioned letter about how getting 100 percent instead of 110 percent on the test was going to ruin my academic career. I would say that she had the patience of a saint, but since I'm not Catholic anymore, let's say that she handled my first of many panic attacks with grace.

I spent most of elementary school in the back of my public-school classroom with my own math and reading assignments. I was hungry for knowledge, and I was indefatigable. This probably has a lot to do with why I became Jewish. Judaism, even more than Catholicism, is a religion rooted in reading and studying, about asking questions to answer them anew.

This tendency to overachieve didn't extend to my catechism studies. I was, for lack of a better phrase, a little shit. Catechism classes took place in the back of the church building, in classrooms that served the community's Catholic K-8 school during the week. The rooms featured white concrete walls and dreary fluorescent lights. The teachers tried to be upbeat and engaging, but many weeks we would end up hunched over workbooks doing fill-in-the-blank Bible stories. Since my dad wasn't there to tell me how many minutes of catechism were left, I passed the time by butchering our weekly art projects and asking questions that made my catechism teachers purse their lips and sigh.

"I don't get it," I announced one day while talking about sin. "If God doesn't want us to sin so badly, why don't we just stay in our attics until we die? Then, we haven't committed any wrongs." I was pleased with my solution.

"God doesn't want us to do that," my teacher sighed impatiently. "Because then we can't do good things, either."

"It seems like a gamble," I countered.

"But that's why we have Jesus," my teacher emphasized, "Everyone sins, but Jesus died so that those sins can be forgiven."

"If everyone sins, why would God want to threaten to send everyone to hell? And what about people who don't believe in Jesus?" I asked. I was genuinely curious.

"It's our job to teach them about Jesus," she pressed on, looking fatigued.

"No, it's your job," I pointed out. She was the catechism teacher, after all.

"Let's move on to the Ten Commandments," she interrupted me. "We're going to memorize them this year."

"Why?" I asked as the rest of the class started to giggle conspiratorially. "Moses wrote them on some rocks, right?"

"Whoever recites the Ten Commandments from memory," my teacher said impatiently, "will get to name our class frog." She swept her hand toward the frog that she had lugged to class in a dirty glass habitat. I wrinkled my nose. I wasn't tempted by amphibians.

"Do animals sin? Did the frogs have a frog kind of Jesus, or does our Jesus also work for them?"

And on it went, until it was time for our parents to drag us to Mass. I don't think I was asking questions to be a pest but because it seemed like Catholicism had a stock answer to every question, and I needed to poke around the edges a bit. Notably, this type of question asking is a cherished Jewish tradition. The Talmud is basically a text of intergenerational debates about Jewish topics, many of which don't have one clear answer in the end. The *Haggadah* that my husband and I use for Passover invites readers to "kick the tires" by asking tough questions about the story of Exodus. I've rarely gone to a Jewish study session that doesn't devolve into spirited arguing. While most churches welcome questions to an extent, Judaism makes a full-on sport out of it. Arguing in pairs is a common feature of Jewish study programs, but my Catechism teacher was not down to be my *chaver*, the person with whom one could study and argue.

For what it's worth, I found the elementary-school curriculum on forgiveness, charity, and prayer to be reasonable and inspiring. It was heaven that I wasn't so sure about. The thing that I fixated on was that non-Christians were allegedly not going to heaven. It seemed arbitrary. You were either born into a Christian family or not based on no merits of your own. It didn't seem like a "free will" issue so much as a "birth and geography" situation. At a rudimentary level, I grasped that in some countries, non-Christian religions predominated. It seemed unfair that those people would have to give up their culture to convert to the religion I'd been born into by chance. I decided quietly and privately that maybe many religions were right. Maybe Jesus wasn't *the* way, the truth, and the light, but *one* particular way, truth, and light. Maybe our paths to God looked different because we were trying to reach the same destination from different starting points. This theory was not Catechism-approved, but I stuck with it.

In order to tease out my belief system, I craved more options. I needed less time to pray silently to a deity whose contours I didn't fully grasp. I needed more space to hear what my gut was trying to suggest about God and the universe. I needed the flexibility to ask difficult questions and leave them unanswered, or as we sometimes do in Judaism, put three answers on the table and commit to none of them as the ultimate truth. In the Church, sometimes we don't trust children enough with that sort of ambiguity. We think that we need to take one answer and cram it down their throats before they're old enough to push back. In the end, that approach didn't work for me, and it doesn't work for many, many of my peers. We can't always control if our kids stay or go when it comes to a particular religious path, but perhaps we can give them a little more room to maneuver while they figure it out.

Like most kids, I didn't have much of a say in the matter. I was dropped off at catechism with my Bible workbook and a flowery skirt and had to make it work. None of my behavior resulted in my being kicked out. I had to attend catechism until I was officially confirmed as a member of the Catholic Church at the end of eighth grade.

In the days leading up to the confirmation ceremony, I refused to pick a confirmation saint because "none of them really gelled with me," whatever that means. There are, of course, female saints, but I couldn't see myself in any of them. I flipped through textbooks and saint-themed trading cards with my eyes glazing over before giving up and not choosing one at all. (I felt the opposite when I picked my Hebrew name—I connected very deeply with the Biblical figure whose name I took on and wrote a passionate essay about her to my *beit din*). I was confirmed nonetheless. They even let me read to the class from The Book of Job. This wasn't because I was an example of piety but because I was the only person who could read in front of a crowd without stumbling over the text of the King James Version of the Bible. I have a photo of me, my skinny frame hidden beneath a modest skirt and blouse, standing several inches away from the attending bishop and offering a shiny, braces-laden smile. My parents might have been proud, but I think they were mostly relieved that we no longer had to keep up with the routine of going to Church each month.

There was something about that bait-and-switch that didn't work for me. When I got my driver's license, the first thing that I did—besides taking myself to the Wendy's drive-thru after cheerleading practice for a Frosty twice a week—was drive myself to Mass at the local church on Sundays and throw a fit that my parents wouldn't join me. I still thought Mass was boring, but I had started to feel that nagging sense of Catholic guilt telling me that if I was in bed instead of Mass, I could count on a one-way ticket to hell later on. I spent most of my high school years attending Mass alone with a dramatic huff, or dragging my very unimpressed, decidedly unreligious father with me. My dad would spend the hour-long Mass staring serenely at the ceiling, as if in a very alluring daydream, or else poking me in the ribs making jokes while I tried to pay attention, like I used to do to him in the sanctuary of St. Thomas the Apostle.

My mom would sit in our rocking chair at home with a Dunkin Donuts cinnamon roll, relishing her chance to have the house to herself before my father and I returned home. When I asked if she wanted to come to Christmas Eve Mass or Easter Sunday services, she made an excuse to avoid even that. One day, as my father and I sat alone at Christmas Eve Mass surrounded by happy Catholic families, I asked him whether he believed in God at all.

"Definitely not," he said with a small smirk, tapping his toe lazily against the wooden kneeler attached to the pew in front of us.

"Then why do you come to Mass?" I demanded.

"You make me," he chuckled.

I didn't make him after that.

CHAPTER 3

"Your beliefs don't make you a better person.
Your behavior does." —*Shukhraj Dhillon*

Since my parents were wholly unsupportive of my newfound devotion, I doubled down and joined my best friend Maria's Catholic youth group. The youth group was a high-energy place where I spent two hours on Monday nights making friends and involving myself in community service.

I also tricked myself into thinking that I had to be a Republican to be a decent Catholic, which made my mother grit her teeth in annoyance. As a catechism student, I had garnered that the "point" of Christianity was to be really nice to people during life and go to heaven to spend eternity with Jesus after death. In youth group, the plan for how to be a good Catholic here on earth was a little more involved. It required plenty of community service, but also dressing modestly, avoiding sex, encouraging those of voting age to vote for "pro-life" candidates, and attending Mass every Sunday because skipping for no reason was a sin. My parents must have missed that memo.

The first youth group event that I attended was a homeless outreach program in Detroit. We met at a suburban church at 5:30 in the morning to assemble sandwiches, which we drove to the corner of Martin Luther King Jr. Boulevard to hand out to the assembled crowd. Feeding the hungry is a central command of Christianity, and I think a very good one. Because Christianity doesn't have as many ritual practices for the home as Judaism, community service becomes the chief way that Christians can physically exercise their faith.

Many white teens in the Detroit suburbs spend very little time in Detroit. Other than venturing to a Tigers game or visiting an older sibling at Wayne State University, a sizable number of us had no ties to the city itself. I knew that my parents had grown up in Detroit and had left for a "better life in the suburbs." I didn't yet have context for the ways in which white flight had driven the high levels of inner-city poverty that we were putting a Band-Aid on with free food and clothes. Band-Aids have their place, of course. Every person needs to be fed and clothed, and this program was a way to meet that need. And to be clear, some Jewish community service also looks like this; I have twice participated in food outreach programs through my synagogue. The problem was that we were taught to "do the work" without thinking more systemically about how to get at the root of the problem.

Our job was to pile up tables of food and clothing for distribution and then pick a station to serve at all morning. The street corner that we served on was a parking lot flanked on both sides by a highway. We were given warnings about Detroit being dangerous on our drive over. We used copious amounts of hand sanitizer, as if Detroit itself could make us ill. Instead of using community service as an opportunity to build relationships and genuine compassion, it felt very much like a "get in and get out" operation.

Maria and I spent the morning matching children and adults to appropriately sized gloves and jackets. As I held up tiny hands to fluffy mittens, I danced in place to stay warm. The crowd was larger than I had anticipated. I kept sorting mittens and bouncing in place as the morning turned into early afternoon. When it was time to pack up, the extra clothes and long plastic tables were returned to our waiting vans, and the parking lot returned to its original state: just gravel and telephone poles, like we had never been there. We gathered in a circle to say a prayer.

I felt pretty righteous. My toes were numb from hours of standing in the cold, and my eyelids were drooping from having woken up so early. I had to be one step closer to admission to heaven at this point. Undeniably, there were a lot of Detroiters in need of food and warm clothes. In that sense, the activity was fundamentally good. I didn't realize until college, though, that what Detroiters needed more was structural change that had long been stymied by institutional racism in the region. We needed a traveling soup kitchen *and* a lengthy conversation about antiracism.

Our volunteerism was more about showing everyone how we followed the Gospel than it was about understanding why it was that so many people who lived but twenty minutes from us didn't have enough food to eat. Driving us to Detroit was also about "showing us how lucky we are" not to live in poverty and to "spread the love of Jesus." Even if I warmed up hundreds of little hands that day, the community service was ultimately about me—what I was learning, what I was gaining.

The issue, of course, is framing. We should be centering the needs of those being served rather than the experience of those serving. It's not that Jewish organizations always get this perfectly right. I didn't convert because Jews are inherently better at community service. But I suspect that high school Shannon understood something that she wasn't ready to verbalize: when you go through life thinking about spreading your religion and getting to heaven, you end up focusing on the wrong things. It was a tiny red flag that I tucked in the back of my mind.

I was too young to question the program, and my parents were probably happy to see me doing something ostensibly more useful than walking around Laurel Park Place Mall. While my mom didn't mind me driving out to Detroit to pass out mittens, she did draw the line at the "homeless experience" sleepover designed to expose us to the hardship of sleeping outside in a cardboard box overnight. We raised some money to be donated to a soup kitchen, which is good, but the concept of asking privileged kids to sleep in boxes with piles of quilts from home and bellies full of their parents' dinner was too surreal for her to bear. I was secretly glad not to have a permission slip for that event. Not because I was worried about sleeping in a box, but because I suspected that something about the event was grotesquely performative.

I recently asked my friend Raechel, who is more experienced with community aid and organizing, to weigh in on these types of religious experiments. She described this type of activity as "poverty tourism," a performative exercise that appeals to emotions without offering structural critiques that can perpetuate solidarity and real systematic change. Maybe the politics of housing were discussed at the event. Based on my friends' stories, however, they mostly had pillow fights.

The highlight of the youth group year was our week-long summer trip to the Appalachian Mountains in rural Pennsylvania, where we provided free housework to local residents. To the host organization's credit, they lived and worked in the area and had longstanding relationships with the county's residents. There was a lot of emphasis on conservation, which made a lasting impact on the way that I thought about resources like fresh water. We talked about God calling us Catholics to take care of the poor and the earth—both noble ideals. We did talk at some length about "doing the work" in order to go to heaven and how "close to Jesus" we felt when we helped people. That kind of ulterior motive is where community service can go off the rails a bit. It was, again, centering the benefits to me instead of the benefits to the community.

I do not write this to disparage community organizing and charity. We should all do as many good deeds as we have the time and energy for. I like to think that a lot of my charity work was time well spent because people were fed and wheelchair ramps were built, and those things need to get done. But somehow, this model of community service left me thinking too much about myself and not enough about the systems that we needed to dismantle in order to create a just world.

In addition to community service, our youth group placed a great emphasis on the great duo of Catholic social issues: opposing abortion and keeping oneself pure for marriage. I went from not knowing what abortion involved to being passionately anti-abortion in less than three weeks. Our youth group invited a pro-life advocate to visit our Monday night meeting armed with tiny plastic embryos for us to *ooh* and *ahh* over. The abortion meeting was always a staple of the youth group calendar. Notably, I don't recall ever inviting a guest speaker to opine on the death penalty, nor on immigration, nor the fact that public school children in Detroit were sitting in crumbling classrooms without enough textbooks. Those issues are all part of broader Catholic social teaching, but I only remember hearing about the tragedy of *Roe v. Wade*.

"What if," I asked during the abortion lecture, "There's something really wrong with your baby? What if it's not going to live for that long?"

"Even if a baby lives for an hour," my youth group leader explained resolutely, "that baby can be a blessing."

It didn't sound like a blessing that I wanted to receive myself, but what did I know?

"Can't some pregnancies be really dangerous?" I asked. "What if the woman is in danger?"

"Her doctors should do everything possible to save both the mom and the baby," my youth group leader responded.

"What if they can't?" I asked curiously.

"We believe in miracles," she said. The conversation was over.

I was onto something with my questions, but the Church had an answer for everything. It was easy to believe the "no excuses" message when I was 16 and living in a comfortable suburban bubble. I didn't dwell on what would happen to the people who desperately needed abortions and couldn't access them. Judaism, I would later learn, tends to think a lot more about the life and well-being of the pregnant person than the rights of the yet-to-be-born child. The majority of movements of Judaism support a person's right to seek an abortion in a variety of circumstances, or at the very least recognize that it's a decision that needs to be made privately. The books I read during the conversion process emphasized repeatedly that the life and health of a pregnant person, both physical and emotional, is really important in Judaism. Judaism's focus on seeing everyone as whole, autonomous people with complex physical and emotional needs was deeply healing to me.

Not yet understanding nuance, I signed up to take the annual bus trip to the March for Life in Washington, D.C. If my mother was concerned about my new anti-choice activism, she did nothing more than purse her lips while signing the permission slip. I believe that I attended the March for Life twice. It's a bit of a blur. We attended a Mass with thousands of other Catholics and then marched up and down the streets of D.C., wrapped in scarves and bearing signs reading things like "abortion kills a person." Even then, I knew that the annual march was not going to change the law, but I liked being part of a screaming crowd. It was a thrill, regardless of what I did or didn't understand about abortion.

"Do you know what women do when they can't get an abortion?" a college classmate asked me within a few months of me arriving on campus.

"Go to a pregnancy center and get help?" I suggested.

"No," she said sharply, "They really, really hurt themselves. They attempt an at-home abortion in ways that risk their lives. You can't stop people from aborting; you can only stop them from aborting safely."

"Oh," I said softly.

It didn't take long for my stance on abortion to crumble. When I was old enough to vote in my first Presidential election, I voted to re-elect Barack Obama in lieu of his pro-life challenger. I wondered if I had become a bad Catholic.

If I wasn't a bad Catholic at the polls, I certainly became a bad Catholic in the bedroom. When I was a teen, there were videos circulating around Christian circles comparing non-virgins to old tape or chewed gum. I saw them at some point, though not at youth group. The metaphor is that if you keep "sticking" yourself to people other than your spouse, your tape will eventually run out of "stick." I took this to mean that my vagina would stop working, but I imagine the metaphor was trying to speak to emotional connection. I'm not going to look it up. The gum metaphor was a little more straightforward. Once you're chewed up and spit out, no one will want you anymore. The video didn't address the fact that we would presumably have sex more than once with our husbands, so I'm not sure where the chewing and spitting come in temporally. Our sex life wasn't something for us to explore and enjoy but something to save and use to serve our spouse. I never took a purity pledge or anything quite so formal, but for my yet nonexistent husband's sake, I vowed to wait.

The nice man who spoke at the National Catholic Youth Conference circa 2009 told us an impassioned tale about how he had saved the "gift" of his virginity for his wife.

"I was so excited to have sex for the first time on my wedding night," he gushed, "I knew that I had saved a precious gift for my wife, and that it would be hers forever." His eyes twinkled.

"I did not remain pure before marriage," his wife chimed in, roaming around the stage in her flowy white blouse, frowning faintly, "And I regretted that." She never said *how* she regretted it, only that she did.

"Our sex life is very rewarding," the man assured the crowd. "All because I had patience and trusted God." I wondered how her husband could be so sure of their sexual compatibility when he didn't have any other experience to draw on, but I took for granted that as long as you loved someone, sex would feel fine.

A friend of mine, in reflecting on similar experiences, wondered why adults thought that we cared about how satisfying their sex lives were. A good question, indeed. I left the conference feeling largely confused about their presentation but convinced that waiting was best.

It wasn't very hard to stay a young virgin in high school. I viewed love as a prerequisite for sex, and I did not love my 16-year-old boyfriends. I barely made an effort to text them back. It didn't necessarily get harder in college. If you've made out with one drunken frat boy on a couch, you've made out with them all. I never really struggled with "temptation," as the Christians call it. Maybe this was because of a mental block instilled by purity culture. It also could have been low sex drive created by general anxiety and exhaustion. But at 20 years old and still a virgin, I started to worry that I was missing out on something that seemed to add joy and connection to the lives of my sexually active peers.

"Do you ever feel *bad* about having sex?" I asked a Jewish woman in my dorm freshman year.

"Bad about what?" she asked, her brow furrowed in confusion.

"Bad that you had sex with someone and you're not, you know, still together."

"No," she shrugged. "Relationships don't have to last forever, they just have to be good while they last."

She wasn't wrong. Perhaps it wasn't the length of the relationship that mattered but the ability of the relationship to provide security and mutual satisfaction for as long as it lasted. In *The Ethical Slut*, Hardy and Easton suggest that we live in a society where "sex is a commodity, a coin you trade for something else—stability, children, a wedding ring—and that any other transaction constitutes being *cheated* and *robbed*." Whether intentionally or not, that's the view that I'd internalized. If I "gave away" sex and didn't get something akin to long-term commitment in return, I was being robbed of something despite that fact that I gave it freely. The end goal for every relationship, whether it involves sex or not, doesn't have to be permanency. As long as we're treating our partners with care and communicating responsibly, it's possible to enjoy short-term arrangements as much as long-term commitment.

My sexually active peers seemed happy, even if the Church would have me believe that they were secretly miserable or headed down a road to inevitable regret and shame. Sex, even casual sex, wasn't leaving my friends in physical or emotional ruin. They didn't seem to have sex as a way to cure low self-esteem. They didn't feel robbed. If there was shame and regret to be had, it was originating with the Church, not in the hearts and minds of my peers. The Church's message had never seemed so contrived. Despite this, I couldn't shake the feelings of shame and anxiety. I usually avoided being alone with male peers at parties because I didn't want to have to negotiate sexual boundaries. I once escaped from a frat boy's room when he went to the bathroom because I didn't know how far he wanted to take the hookup and I felt incapable of asking. I made it to junior year without having done much more than kiss a boy.

There was so much pressure around the concept of virginity that my first time seemed like an inordinately large deal. I started desperately wanting to get the first time over with, and I wanted to do it as soon as possible. I was, at the time, enrolled in a course about Armenian history. It was an early morning class, but I didn't mind because it happened to be filled with very handsome men. When we took a field trip to a local Armenian museum, a gorgeous Lebanese classmate sat next to me on the bus.

"I'm Joey," he introduced himself, popping his earbuds out of his ears and making unwavering eye contact with me.

"I'm Shannon," I smiled back, awkwardly offering him my hand.

"I know," he said flatly.

"Oh," I giggled shyly.

"You gave your book report last week," he explained. "It was the best one in the class. You're highly competent."

"Thank you," I said, blushing and biting my lip. Competent was a good start. His directness and confidence drew me in immediately. We made small talk all day and walked around the museum. I looked favorably upon his candidacy as a potential sexual partner.

"Do you want to hang out some time?" Joey asked casually as we hopped off the bus and back into the cold Michigan air.

"Yes, I'd like that a lot," I agreed with a coy smile. Mission success.

"I just went through a breakup," he warned me, "so I can't be in another relationship."

"That's fine, I don't have time for a boyfriend," I assured him.

"I'm also an atheist," he said, staring distastefully at my cross necklace.

"No matter," I assured him.

My new not-boyfriend was whip smart and very bossy. Joey had dark brown eyes, and his smile was always a little devious. His room was filled with chemistry textbooks that he pored over all day. He wanted to go to medical school. Joey also had his own espresso machine, which is an underrated way to win over sexual partners.

By his telling, he'd had sex with about a dozen people. Contrary to popular wisdom, that didn't make him a predator or a jerk. Let's just say that you could tell that he was well-practiced. We watched a basketball game together at my house for our first not-date. Later that week he invited me to spend the night before our class. I knew that he wasn't after a casual sleepover. I said yes.

As it turns out, virginity is somewhat of a dud as a gift. I, like many women having sex for the first time, mostly lay there like a dead fish.

"Ow," I hissed as he entered me very slowly. "This kind of hurts."

"It's just the tip," he informed me clinically. "Let me know if you want me to pause."

"Oh," I replied. "It's okay, keep going."

He did. After a minute or so, it didn't hurt any more, but it didn't feel fantastic, either. He seemed to pick up on my lack of enthusiasm.

"I think we should stop," he suggested, "I don't want you to be sore tomorrow."

"Ok," I agreed. "It didn't hurt that bad." It wasn't exactly a rave review. The mechanics had worked, but I wasn't understanding the appeal quite yet.

He didn't seem offended.

"The first time can be like that," he conceded, rolling over to his side of the bed. "We need to go to bed. I have an alarm set for 7:30."

"Okay, well, thank you ..." I said awkwardly. I felt like he had done me some sort of favor by walking me through my first time, however clinically.

"Sleep," he said flatly. His tone brokered no room for argument. I grabbed for the covers and willed myself to get tired.

"I don't feel like chewed gum," I mumbled softly to the ceiling as Joey drifted off to sleep.

"Did you say something?" Joey asked, rolling back over and staring at me blankly.

"No," I lied. I rolled in the opposite direction and closed my eyes.

He didn't ask again.

I woke up in a good mood, happy to have gotten the first time behind me. Joey even made me eggs for breakfast, along with a double-shot of espresso from his fancy machine, so you can't say he wasn't polite about the whole thing. I couldn't stop thinking, *why would anyone want this awkward, painful first-time sex to happen on their wedding night?!*

On my actual wedding night, I made Travis pry fifty bobby pins out of my head, and I fell asleep after eating a couple of chocolate truffles. *L'chaim*, I guess.

After Joey, there were a few other college flings. The guy on the baseball team who was always drinking whole milk straight from the gallon and asking me why I wouldn't partake. The frat boy who thought it was strange but somewhat funny that I brought my own condoms to the bar the night that we met. The political science classmate with whom I arranged a late-night hookup in the library stacks. The woman into BDSM who was prone to giving long lectures on religion and shame while I stared blankly out of her car window. The Chaldean man with a magical laugh who gave excellent shoulder massages. Each encounter gave me new information about what I enjoyed and how I related to my partners. In turn, I used that information to exercise agency and be vocal about my needs. My standards became higher as I learned more about consent and pleasure, not lower. I had sex when I wanted to and abstained when I didn't.

Every "yes" became more enthusiastic and every "no" less apologetic.

I was fortunate to have partners who were invested in making sure that both participants consented enthusiastically and had a good time. We understood our respective roles in preventing unwanted pregnancy and STDs. Everyone managed not to treat me like gum or tape or another strange, inanimate object. As I learned how to love my sex life, I was also learning how to love myself. This phase of my life is filled with positive memories, not regrets. I think Travis is glad that I entered our marriage knowing what I wanted out of our sex life. He has never expressed the slightest bit of disappointment that he missed the boat on a total monopoly on my vagina. He reports that my tape is very much sticky. Neither of us know what that means.

Even if Jewish tradition frowns upon extramarital sex, my Jewish friends were unfamiliar with the type of purity culture that young Christians grow up with. In an unofficial survey of Jewish friends conducted via text message, purity is not a constant fixation of what it means to be a Jewish teen. I asked my friends if they'd ever seen any videos about virginity like the ones I'd described, and they assured me that they had not.

"Jews are allowed to get divorced and remarried," Alana explained, "So, I don't think the chewed gum thing would fit in with Jewish beliefs. Also, that sounds gross."

"We focus a lot more on consent and safety," my rabbi's wife explained over the phone. "Yes, we want them to know that sex is something that is serious and can be intense emotionally, but you can't tell teenagers not to have sex and omit all of the information about how to do it safely. Some Jews might prefer not to talk about it because of the belief that sex should only take place in the context of marriage, but we've largely moved away from relying on an abstinence-based model."

Officially, the United Synagogue of Conservative Judaism *opposes* abstinence-based sex education. Judaism also generally permits sex for pleasure rather than solely for procreation. And the Jewish method seems to be working. In an essay about Judaism and sex, Gloria Feldt says that, "Jews have fewer unintended pregnancies, teen pregnancies, and abortions than most Americans of other faiths. This is in no small part because Judaism has a... more realistic sexual ethic than the more conflicted one that pervades American culture." Feldt emphasizes that Jews are clear-eyed about "both the value of sex and its potential for causing problems."

I think that most religious adults know that abstinence-based sex education doesn't work, just like they know that if they presented two sides to the conversation of abortion, you might have some dissenters in your ranks. The key to all of this youth group socialization is not only that we become teenagers who shun sex and advocate against abortion. The key is that you become *othered*. You become the teen who secretly or not-so-secretly thinks that you're better than all of your "slutty," birth control-using classmates. You become someone who thinks that your only home is in the church because the people "out there" are living lives of sin and immorality. We know from social science research that being othered is a powerful way to reinforce your commitment to the "ingroup."

Once, our high school accelerated English class had a debate about stem cell research. The official Catholic stance was that "no objective, even though noble in itself, such as a foreseeable advantage to science, to other human beings or to society, can in any way justify experimentation on living human embryos or fetuses, whether viable or not." The rest of the class declared stem cell research a wonderful idea and set down their debate handouts, hoping to pass the rest of our hour together in peace. Maria and I would have none of it. We argued fervently against the immorality of stem cell research while the rest of the class doodled uncomfortably. At our prayer group the next week, we proudly professed that we had been the only ones standing up for the embryos. I never understood what stem cell research actually entailed, but I understood that I was definitely in the right.

By the time that I arrived as a freshman at the University of Michigan, I somehow identified not as a reluctant Catholic who had been a dunce in Sunday School, but as a staunch adherent to the faith who would show up to Mass every Sunday with a smile on my face and my long, tangled brown hair in a neat, polished ponytail. I felt good going to Mass every week. Part of this was genuine. Having an hour for quiet reflection where I wasn't studying, partying, or trying to make the library printer cooperate was a precious gift. Another part of this was that attending Mass allowed me to feel like I existed on a higher spiritual plane than my peers, most of whom fled their religious obligations the second they arrived on campus.

It's impressive that I rode the wave of youth-group-era enthusiasm as long as I did. When the spell started to wear off, I was too numb to my habits to consider a change. Maybe it was fear of being sent to hell or fear of having been wrong about God and God's rules. I couldn't put my finger on what was off, so I kept going through the motions, desperate to keep myself away from the hellfire of cynicism and nonbelief.

Judaism waited patiently to show me where I belonged instead.

CHAPTER 4

"The secret of change is to focus all of your
energy not on fighting the old, but on building
the new." −*Socrates*

Before going to college, I knew that Judaism existed,
but only vaguely. I understood on some level that Jesus
was a Jew, but what that meant for me as a Catholic was
less clear.

One girl on my gymnastics team was Jewish. She
might have been the only Jew I knew throughout my
childhood. I only found out because our coaches made her
a blue-and-gold "Happy Hanukkah" poster one year when
the rest of us got "Merry Christmas" banners and because
her mother couldn't attend gymnastics competitions that
took place on Saturday, the Jewish Sabbath. She didn't talk
much about it. From what I could tell, being Jewish meant
not being Christian. Later, my high school government
teacher married a Jewish man. A rabbi had performed
their wedding in a helicopter. It sounded pretty cool, but
it only taught me that out there somewhere was a rabbi

who was not very afraid of heights. Of Judaism itself, I still knew almost nothing.

In college, I was stunned to find out that tons of my classmates and professors were Jewish. I had no idea about Jewish summer camp or the various Jewish organizations that existed on campus. I didn't have many Yiddish-isms in my vocabulary. I had seen Yom Kippur, a major Jewish holiday focusing on atonement, on various secular calendars, but what it involved I was unaware of. Being thrust into a world where most people had gone their whole lives without hearing about the love of Jesus was a startling change of pace.

At the time, I was fairly active at St. Mary's Student Parish, a wonderful student-oriented Catholic church near campus. St. Mary's was homey and inviting. The interior of the church was rather spartan, but the lounge featured fluffy couches and sometimes free cookies. St. Mary's was different from the church affiliated with my youth group in every possible way. I never heard a priest talk about abortion or sex. The staff focused on the annual warming shelter, which provided valuable assistance to individuals without stable housing during the brutal Michigan winters. The church threw significant resources at stopping deportations of local community members, a mission that I supported. I was proud to be a member. Sunday evening Mass was a place to be quiet and contemplative. It was a break from the loud party-going weekend ventures and the buzz of classroom discussion. People describe St. Mary's as a "liberal" parish because members of the Ann Arbor community who attend services are ostensibly progressive politically. But in Catholicism, which is nothing if not bureaucratic, it doesn't necessarily mean anything that the parishioners identify as progressive. As far as I know, the church doesn't perform gay weddings, and a priest once admitted to refusing to baptize the child of an unmarried woman. The uncomfortable issues that I ignored about the church were always there, vibrating constantly in the background.

I went to Mass every week, but I didn't meet many other Catholic students. I would occasionally see acquaintances from classes or my dormitory, and I would offer a nonintrusive smile and wave as we settled into our separate pews. I never experienced Mass as a social affair. Most of the classmates that I actually spent time with were Jewish.

Jewish students seemed to have a community connection that the Catholic community lacked, even at our warm, welcoming parish. There was interesting diversity in the observance of my Jewish classmates, from students who strictly kept kosher to students who openly admitted that they had no faith in God but enjoyed eating apples and honey for Rosh Hashanah, the Jewish New Year. I was fascinated by all of it. I wanted to ask questions and absorb their answers. And so began the tiny spark that would eventually grow into the motivation for my conversion. I was curious about Judaism, sure, but the curiosity was more like a gravitational pull that I couldn't describe. I strongly considered joining a Jewish sorority, but I had no idea why I wanted to do that so badly. I ended up choosing a sorority that had a mix of

Jewish and Christian members. When people pulled me aside on campus to ask if I was Jewish in hopes of getting me to join their student organization, I was always a little disappointed to have to say no. When a Chabad volunteer offered me a *hamantaschen* [triangular cookies filled with jam or poppy seeds] on Purim, I was delighted that he had confused me for a Jewish student. I almost applied to work at my friend's Jewish summer camp before deciding that I would be an outcast there. I Googled whether non-Jewish kids could go to Jewish summer camp, already thinking about which one I would pick for my future offspring. Every Magen David necklace on campus caught my eye. The magnetic draw toward Judaism is something that I can't explain though I suspect other converts would relate to the feeling. Judaism was a whisper, an itch. It was saying something to my soul that I wasn't yet ready to hear. I responded by peppering my Jewish classmates with questions, which they answered graciously.

One of my sorority sisters once told me, while choosing an outfit for the High Holidays, "I don't have any faith, but I was invited to high holiday services at Chabad and I'm going to go."

"Why do you want to go to the service, then?" I asked, more confused than judgmental. "Tell me about the services. What happens? What are they like?"

"I don't know," she answered honestly, thumbing through her wardrobe for a reasonably modest dress. "I guess it reminds me of home. My family always went to services on Yom Kippur. I don't believe in God, but I'm always going to be Jewish. And as for the service... you kind of stand there all day and people pray in Hebrew."

I was fascinated. Christian students often arrive on campus eager to get away from their parents' version of religion, while Jewish students seemed to cling to their culture more. Judaism wasn't merely a set of metaphysical beliefs; it was a culture and identity unto itself. Yiddish phrases were thrown around by Ashkenazi Jews, and Jewish parents sent care packages with honey cakes for Rosh Hashanah. There were shared experiences with summer camp and Jewish youth organizations. I had my first bagel and lox with a Jewish friend, and I learned to groan *"oy vey"* when things weren't going my way. My Jewish friends were gracious enough to include me in their culture in the most non-pushy way imaginable. I asked a few people if I could come to services with them, and they always cheerfully said "sure" but then never brought it up again unless I persisted. It's not that they didn't want me to come along but that to be pushy about it would feel unnatural to them.

I also had a penchant for developing crushes on my Jewish classmates. One of my would-be boyfriends, Robbie, spent his summers working at a Jewish summer camp. He was clearly proud to be Jewish, but I'd never heard him talk about going to services even once. In the dining hall during Passover, Robbie made his way over to the matzoh pizza station while telling me about all of the dietary laws related to the holiday. Wanting to be polite, I set my tray down beside his and copied what he was doing.

"Wait, you don't have to do that," Robbie insisted, carefully spreading sauce on his thin, crumbling matzoh. "You can eat whatever you want. It won't offend me."

"No, I want to," I insisted, "What do I put on it?" The matzoh pizza station was being swarmed by other students, but I wasn't understanding the appeal. It looked like a lackluster lunch.

"Jews don't mix milk and meat, so basically you can use whatever vegetables you want with the cheese," he explained, "Also, pepperoni is a pork product. We don't eat pork, either." I looked at the other presumably Jewish students crowding the matzoh pizza station.

"That kid is eating deli turkey with his cracker pizza," I pointed out. An unconventional combination, but not the weirdest thing one could see in a dining hall.

"Stop calling it a cracker pizza. It's matzoh. And not everyone keeps kosher," Robbie explained.

"But why make a matzoh pizza if you don't keep kosher?" I pressed. "Why not make a turkey sandwich?"

"There are ... I guess there are different levels of kosher," he tried to explain. "It's complicated. He might mix milk and meat but not eat leavened bread during Passover. Maybe he likes matzoh pizza. I don't know."

"It's not that complicated," I conceded. "I'll eat what you eat."

It really didn't seem too complicated to me. Judaism was not an all-or-nothing kind of religion. There were fewer impassioned accusations of cherry-picking if adherents chose to keep kosher but not observe the Sabbath, if they follow some of the laws of keeping kosher but not others, or if they show up to a Rosh Hashanah service for nothing other than nostalgia. There was so much room to breathe.

I had another crush on Ian, a blond, curly-haired Jewish classmate in my intro to philosophy class. I didn't understand his religious practice. He seemed to not care much about the spiritual dimensions of Judaism and loudly exclaimed, "Horseshit!" when I tried to convince him that Jesus really must have risen from the dead. He talked fondly and intelligently about some aspects of Judaism, but for him, it was clear that Judaism was a family and collective culture more than something to take literally. To him, observing a religion and affiliating with it were different matters entirely.

"Oh, you're really observant," Ian remarked as I sadly picked pieces of cold grilled chicken off of my salad. It was a Friday during Lent, when many observant Catholics avoid meat.

"I mean, what would be the point if not?" I asked dismissively. "Why be Catholic and blow off Lent?"

"I personally love bacon cheeseburgers," Ian offered. (Bacon, for the uninitiated, is not kosher, nor is mixing dairy and meat).

"Because Judaism is more cultural than Catholicism," I conceded. "There's no point in being Catholic if you don't, you know, believe Catholic things."

"I'm positive that there are people who are culturally Catholic but not observant," Ian suggested.

"I guess," I said thoughtfully, twirling my fork around in my Caesar dressing and racking my brain for examples of such people. "My internship supervisor this summer was Italian Catholic and wasn't religious. She associated Catholicism with her family's heritage, but she was a jerk. So, I don't think the whole cultural Catholic vibe was working for her."

"Well, being religious and being a good person are separate issues," Ian laughed.

"Cultural Judaism feels different from cultural Catholicism," I explained, taking a sip of iced coffee and leaning against the wall next to me. "There's no particular community cohesion between Catholics and non-practicing former Catholics."

"There are far fewer Jews than Christians in the world," Ian explained patiently, "It's a smaller community so there's more cohesion regardless of how spiritual you are."

"Do you want to eat the chicken or not?" I offered, poking the cold strips closer to his side of the table. We left the conversation about religion there and returned to our discussion of philosophy. I'm sure he promptly forgot about the conversation, but it stuck with me. The ability of the Jewish community to stick together despite glaring differences in their beliefs astounded me.

Next, I turned to Google. I spent some of my limited free time sophomore year poking around for information on how one might convert to Judaism. Unfortunately for me, some of the information that you find about conversion on the great wide web is not confidence-inspiring. I read that rabbis would turn me away, that the community would question my conversion, and that unless I planned to unfailingly obey every last commandment in the Torah, I would be a burden on the community. In my experience, none of those things came to be; no one turned me away, and no one has ever accused me of being a burden on the community. At the time, I had no way of knowing what was true and what was false.

I berated myself with the fact that I wouldn't be accepted. I convinced myself that you can't be Jewish if you don't have a Jewish grandmother or didn't grow up going to Jewish summer camp. I felt that I could never adequately understand the pain that comes with centuries of religious persecution and exile, so I would constantly be missing out on an understanding of Jewish culture even if I studied the religion.

I was also intimidated by Hebrew. Freshman year, I wrote "Happy Hanukkah" in Hebrew on a gift for my close friend Leah, and it took me nearly ten minutes to match my handwriting on the package to the Hebrew script on Google Translate. I was already studying Arabic and trying to retain enough of my high school German to get by. My brain was full to exploding with language. I tried to be reasonable with myself: conversion was too difficult, and I needed to stick with what I knew.

The familiar is powerful. Mass was peaceful, predictable, orderly. I kept going, and I did get something out of it. The homilies were often thoughtful, and I slept well on Sunday nights after experiencing the soothing music in the darkness of St. Mary's basement at nine p.m. Mass. The thing that continued to plague me was loneliness. It was hard to stop myself from noticing that the environment at Mass could be a little stiff. Unlike Jews, who will bond almost instantly over their shared culture, Catholics don't always see themselves as inherently having much in common. Getting a warm smile at Mass was a win; having a conversation in the hallways after Mass rarely ever happened. Perhaps it's because when Mass ended it was almost ten p.m., but the situation wasn't much better when I managed to get to ten a.m. Mass. I almost always went alone and left alone. When I started attending Mass with several of my teammates from the cheerleading team, this loneliness abated, but I never really found the communal warmth and connection that I was looking for. I decided that I must not be trying hard enough. When all else fails, blame yourself. If Jews could build community on campus, Catholics could, too.

In an effort to "get involved," I signed up to teach catechism classes once a month to elementary school students. A week before each class, I would meet with fellow student teachers in the church social hall, eating pasta or fish that had been lovingly donated by community members. Free food is a definite benefit of campus ministries. With full bellies, we would huddle over curriculum books and make a lesson plan. They were usually pretty straightforward. A lesson about All Soul's Day, a unit about poverty and hunger, a day devoted to apologies and forgiveness. On the appointed day, I would head to church early for free bagels and trudge up to my second-floor classroom to spread the word. I had a class full of raucous third-grade boys who tossed scissors and laughed about how homelessness was "fun, like camping." I didn't know how to run a classroom, and the questions they asked were deceptively complicated.

"Prayer doesn't work," a tiny blond-haired boy told me during the All Souls' Day class, his face contorted into a frown. "My grandma died, and I pray all the time, but I'm still really sad."

"I'm sorry," I told him, scrambling to figure out how to comfort an 8-year-old about loss. "Sometimes, it takes a lot of time to accept that the person we love is gone. Prayer isn't an instant fix. I promise that as the months and years go by, you'll start to feel better, and it won't hurt so much when you think about your grandma."

"Everyone says you'll get over it eventually," snarled a spiky-haired boy in a soccer jersey. "But then prayer doesn't *really* work. It only helps you pass the time until you feel better anyway."

"I think that prayer works," I sighed. But he was right that prayer doesn't work as a transaction: you can't ask God for happiness and get it back like the heavens are a divine vending machine. Years later, a rabbi at Mishkan Chicago would speak about the purpose of prayer in a way that might have helped me out in this situation. She emphasized that the point of prayer is to meet an emotional need within ourselves. It is in accepting our own helplessness and shouting to the heavens for help that we find catharsis and relief even if we don't expect that the prayer will be answered in a tangible way. When Moses called out to God to heal his sister Miriam, she posited, he wasn't necessarily doing it because he thought that his shouting would move the needle. He was doing it because it felt good. Whatever type of prayer that my third-grade friend had been taught wasn't making him feel better because he had been taught to think about the outcome (God taking away his sadness) and not the experience of prayer (the healing that comes through surrendering to the feelings and crying out for help).

In any case, I wasn't a clergy member, and I was pretty rotten at giving advice. It went like this week after week: the boys resisting my lessons and me babbling anxiously while improvising answers. It was an unmitigated disaster. After two years, I gave up my teaching gig. I briefly considered joining Challah for Hunger, a Jewish student group that baked bread and distributed it to hungry families in the area. Nervous that I wouldn't fit in or that people would be suspicious about my participation, I signed up for a Catholic fall weekend retreat instead, hoping that it would help me make more Catholic friends.

The retreat was fine, but it felt like everyone else already knew each other and I was playing catch up. Being Catholic doesn't give two people a ton to bond over, so I tried my best to find common ground with my fellow retreatants. I managed to make one friend. Zack was interested in dating me. I didn't return his feelings, but he was kind and outgoing. So, we started spending time together. Zack was devoted to the Catholic Church and wanted to make a career of working for Catholic charities. His majors were ancient civilizations and Biblical studies. He told me that he knew so much about Judaism that he could be Jewish himself. I was positive that wasn't how it worked, but I nodded politely.

Zack was in charge of a mission trip to Nicaragua, so I signed up to spend my spring break at a Jesuit compound in Managua. (I know, I know—these mission trips are white saviorism at their worst, but you can't do better until you know better, and I didn't know better). In Nicaragua, our job was to make improvements on an elementary school and spread the love of Jesus to the local children.

When we arrived in Managua and got to work, it quickly became clear that 1) I was useless as a volunteer construction worker, and 2) the children of Nicaragua read their Bibles way more than I did. I propose that they didn't need a skeptical, non-Spanish-speaking Catholic to inspire them. In fact, I admitted that I didn't speak Spanish when I signed up, but I was told that it wouldn't matter. I felt out of place, smiling vacantly at the children as they tried to engage me. A very kind fourth grader sat down one day and rattled off a long list of Spanish vocabulary words to help me keep up. He took my sunglasses as payment. My largest contribution to the trip was that I was a load of fun to play tag with in the relentless 90-degree weather. While my fellow volunteers chatted with older children in the shade, I ran around with the younger kids as they shrieked and giggled in delight. The idea that any of this was teaching the kids about Jesus seemed far-fetched. They were already deeply religious. We were on a field trip designed to entertain and enrich us, but many of my peers seemed to think that we were out there changing the world. The gap between our perspectives was alarming.

Halfway through the week, our local trip leader said that we were going to take a drive through the nearby landfill, where most of the town was employed sorting trash and recyclables under the hot sun.

"Some years they throw trash at the buses," she said, "but don't worry."

"They probably don't want Americans driving down here to gawk at them," one of my fellow volunteers pointed out politely. Her name was Sarah. I felt glad that she had spoken up, and I agreed with her sentiment.

"If it upsets them," I added, "have we thought about... not? We can sit right here on this curb and enjoy our lunch break without disturbing their work day."

"It's important to see how these people live," Zack explained impatiently.

"I think we know exactly how they live," Sarah countered, "And I don't think we should be driving around in an air-conditioned van while the rest of the community walks everywhere they go."

We lost that battle, and the group took a horribly objectifying drive around the trash compound. We won the war on the van, though. The school where we volunteered was nearly 30 minutes from the Jesuit housing where we were staying, so we compromised and had the bus driver leave us on a street corner near the school so that we could spend the rest of the day walking like everyone else. This is a small victory, but it was better than nothing.

On the last day of the trip, the kids insisted on a soccer tournament. They beat us so badly that half of them eventually volunteered to join our team to even out the score. We went home sweaty and having achieved next to nothing. The school bathrooms still didn't work when we left, but I painted them a very charming shade of aqua. We had built about half a sidewalk, but the hired construction crew undoubtedly fixed it up when we were gone. I sensed that we had accomplished very little other than making ourselves feel like heroes. We weren't seeing the communities we served as fully human. We looked at them as stepping stones on our way to heaven; people who helped us act out the role of Jesus, like they'd been hired to fill background roles in the movie of our religious development. I should have joined Challah for Hunger, after all.

After returning home, I gave up on trying to fit into the social life of St. Mary's. I resigned myself to attending Mass and dropping the occasional five dollars in the collection plate. I stayed in touch with Zack until he posted a rant on Facebook about how poor people shouldn't be allowed to buy "fancy" food like steak with public assistance money unless they wanted to "get off of their asses and work like everyone else." This is not exactly the empathy that one would expect of a mission trip leader, but it was unsurprising in a deeply depressing sort of way. I blocked him on Facebook and declared my life as a missionary over. Since Jews don't do mission trips, my embargo on them has gone unchallenged. This is a blessing.

CHAPTER 5

"Crisis means to sift. Let it all fall away and you'll
be left with what matters."
–Glennon Doyle Melton

Eventually, I was lured away from St. Mary's by the promise of a better time. The Hail Mary (no pun intended) for those who no longer feel a connection with the Church is often to find a "fun" church, the kind that opens services with free lattes and pyrotechnics. A bunch of cute male acquaintances attended one such "fun" church near campus. So, instead of wandering over to Hillel or Chabad in the hopes of becoming Jewish, I stayed on the Christian path and signed up to go to what I'll refer to as "Rock Band Church." Rock Band Church was non-denominational, so what they believed was not totally clear at the outset. I knew that they had free donuts, loud music, and lots of single attendees.

For starters, picking a church because cute boys also go to that church is not a great way to find spiritual fulfillment. I went for the boys, and I stayed because the worship band that played on Sundays was really quite good. It was the antithesis of a quiet, orderly Catholic service. They showed funny YouTube videos, and the drumming left my ears with that fuzzy, subdued feeling for hours after I'd left. The first time I went to services, stage lights surrounding the auditorium made it glow blue and purple. The walls were white, and there was one giant wooden cross hanging above the stage, which was covered in the band's equipment. I unbuttoned my coat and took two chocolate donut holes from the table near the front doors. I found a seat next to a friend while the guitarist warmed up. It didn't feel like church, but I wasn't turned off from it, either. Before services began, one of the senior pastors wandered over to introduce himself.

"What brings you to Rock Band Church?" he asked kindly, clapping me on the back with his large hand.

"Oh, some friends invited me," I explained, gesturing to the people seated in my row. "I'm actually Catholic, but I heard you served coffee and I'm fresh out at home." Me and my obsession with free caffeine. He laughed.

"We have a few Catholics in our midst," he assured me. "For some of them, this never feels like church, and for others, they have a lot of fun and get a lot out of the service. I hope you like it."

I nodded politely as he took off to scout out the other newcomers.

As more and more people trickled in, the atmosphere was loud and lively. The room was buzzing with friendly chatter as students socialized in small pods and munched on donuts and granola bars. Service started much like a rock concert: the lights dimmed, and the instruments started up. It eventually got so loud that conversation stopped, and people turned toward the front of the room to join in on the singing.

It wasn't a bad experience. The music was loud, and I could get up to refill my coffee whenever I wanted. The worship songs were punctuated by people getting up to speak. There was the sermon, which the pastor tried to make more relatable by quoting Jesus as if he talked like a millennial teenager. I'm unconvinced that Jesus ever said "dude" or "bro," but I understand the impetus. All in all, the service was longer than Mass but not completely irreverent. I had a decent time and vowed to come back with my friends.

Rock Band Church was very focused on improving its numbers, so once you show up to services, you get roped into small group Bible studies and myriad church events. The church's philosophy was based on the "great commission," as it's called. Jesus allegedly said to "go and make disciples of all nations," which the church took as unfettered permission to push the Christian faith on every unsuspecting student and community member. Because of this, I got plenty of calls, texts, and emails inviting me back. The Catholic Church had never seemed this enthusiastic about my participation, so Rock Band Church won me over with attention and persistence. If nothing else, it is funny that I would eventually join one of the least evangelizing religions possible.

I joined a Bible group full of the nicest women that you can imagine. We shared snacks and read the Bible and talked about our college woes. Once, another woman tried to convince me to ask my curly-haired crush, Ian, what he knew about Jesus, but I tactfully declined. To do so felt like it would violate a boundary and destroy what existed of our friendship. I never regretted attending my Bible study, though, and I had no qualms about game nights or potlucks. Like most college students, I craved social time, even if it was conditional upon my faith in Jesus. Eventually, I was invited to join the church's summer "leadership" program.

"You seem like you would be a great fit," one of the church leaders told me at an event. "It's a program about becoming a leader and finding your voice."

"I already have a job this summer," I told her. "Thanks, anyway."

"It's only part-time," she pressed. "Everyone has a second or even third job."

"What does it involve?" I asked skeptically. Leadership seemed like a vague catch-all term. I wanted to know what else I was getting myself into.

"Basically, you spend time deepening your faith and learning to witness to others, putting yourself out there for Christ." A red flag went up in my brain, and I shifted uncomfortably in my plastic chair.

"It's evangelization," I said. "Going out and inviting people to church?"

"It's not that," she explained. "It's building relationships with people and showing them—" I stopped listening. I had heard about this program. People who had participated in this program were sent out to find hundreds of strangers to question about Jesus and heaven. They interrupted summer porch gatherings and adults reading at coffee shops to engage them in a "survey" about Christianity. The purpose of the survey was to uncover nonbelievers and push them to profess their faith in Jesus. The idea made my insides turn.

"We even have scholarships," the church leader added with a grin.

"You mean people pay to do this program?" I asked incredulously. "It sounds like people are working for the church by bringing in more members. Usually my summer jobs pay me, not the other way around." I was aghast.

"It's a program about you," she said, smiling patronizingly. "It's for your development."

"I'll think about it," I lied.

I never joined the summer program, and I never invited anyone else to church. It didn't feel right.

In order to get new members, the church engaged in something called "love bombing" where current members showered prospective members in support and attention in an effort to get them coming to church regularly. Church leaders were encouraged to help students with laundry or offer them rides to nearby grocery stores in order to get them interested in church involvement. I refused to partake. You're not doing someone a favor if you're hoping for something in return. If you quit the church at any point, you could no longer count on friendly text messages or help with laundry. When one pastor left the church and came out as gay, all of the people that he'd spent 20 years in close relationship with stopped talking to him and deemed him an "enemy" almost overnight. The cruelty of it was unbearable.

In contrast, a campus Jewish student association would bring matzoh ball soup and bread to sick students at their dorms. I asked my friend Leah whether they would bring soup to non-Jews.

"Why not?" she asked.

"I don't know," I said, "Usually those outreach programs have an ulterior motive, like getting people more involved in religious life." I was thinking, obviously, about Rock Band Church.

"The motivation is that sick people like soup," she replied flatly. The simplicity was foreign to me.

I never participated in evangelization on any level, and I was unreliable about "tithing." Tithing is essentially donating to the church, and Rock Band Church asked for ten percent of each member's salary as a suggested monthly or yearly tithe. I want to be clear that I made money by mopping up the West Quad dining hall and keeping the cereal area in order, so I didn't have a ton of money to offer in the first place. After purchasing some Costco-size cases of oatmeal, feminine products, textbooks, and paying my electricity bill, I wasn't often coming out with a surplus at the end of each month.

Even so, I felt compelled to donate to individual church leaders, many of whom were not paid a full salary by the church itself. These quasi-employees were asked to "support-raise," which basically meant raising money for

SHANNON GONYOU

rent, food, and medical care from the ground up. I always felt a surge of annoyance when I got their fundraising emails, thanking God for providing for them each month. It wasn't really God providing for them but students like me, who were often giving out of an almost-empty pot. I had to log two or more hours at the dining hall to cover my donation to them, and God certainly wasn't helping me clean up the daily Cheerio and milk explosion. It never sat well with me, but as long as the church leaders knew what they were signing up for, I decided that it was none of my business.

It took time, but I slowly realized that Rock Band Church was quite different from the faith espoused by the Catholic Church. Every single sermon seemed to focus on how lost and broken we all were without Jesus. Every week, I heard what lowly, hopeless trash we all were without Christ. They billed their faith as beautiful and hopeful because they believed in life after death, but the whole "you're a sinner for life" message was a bit of a downer. A recent version of their website stated that, "Thus, all human beings are born with a corrupted nature and without spiritual life and are totally incapable of pleasing God in themselves." Very heartwarming. Judaism rejecting the idea of original sin was probably the biggest theological relief of all once I started my conversion. That, and the fact that the Conservative Judaism movement ordains women and supports LGBTQ members. Rock Band Church mostly refused to be clear on its beliefs about homosexuality and female leadership. After a lot of kvetching from the community, the church compromised

85

by offering an in-person "intro class" to discuss these issues live instead of posting them on their website.

There were other theological quirks that I hadn't encountered before. People often talked about the devil and evil spirits, which had rarely been a topic of conversation in my Catholic circles. I found it strange and unpleasant to think about demons attacking me all the time. Jews take a hybrid serious-humorous approach to superstition. The demon fear was all business at Rock Band Church. The church also adhered to fairly rigid gender roles, and students were encouraged to think about marriage early. The church pushed people into marriage before they were ready. I saw a painful example of this firsthand—an engagement that came out of left field and was broken off months later to great anguish on both sides.

I didn't particularly want to get married young, but by this point in my college career, I had made out with enough frat boys and was ready to settle down. I was ready for a boyfriend, and Rock Band Church seemed like a good place to find one. The boyfriend I met at church was a nice enough young man. Tom had dark hair and dark brown eyes—just my type—and an adorable collection of sweaters. We made conversation at church a few times, and then I upped the ante by asking him if he wanted to attend my sorority's semiformal with me. He accepted.

Tom was up front about the fact that he wanted a leadership role in his future relationship.

"I want to lead," he told me when we had lunch for the first time. I don't think either of us knew what that meant in practice. According to the church, men and women had distinct roles in relationships, but how that would play out was less clear.

"I want someone who isn't physically aggressive," I admitted. Aim high, I suppose.

"Why would anyone be physically aggressive to their girlfriend?" Tom asked, furrowing his eyebrows and staring at me blankly.

"I don't know," I shrugged, "Alcohol? Insecurity? Some people just are." To his credit, Tom didn't have a temper, and he didn't drink. He was remarkably laid-back and chipper.

Predictably, our relationship never was perfect, but according to our friends, we made it look perfect. We were smiley and gentle with one another in public, we showed up to each other's performances, and we spent a ton of time together, both at church events and elsewhere. Tom carried umbrellas for me when it was raining, and I always bought him a heart-shaped ice cream cake for Valentine's Day. When things were going well, we were best friends. When we had free time on campus, we would drive to the local mega-theater to watch a late-night flick over shared popcorn, or we would gather with friends to watch Michigan basketball games.

It took me longer than expected to win over his friends. It seemed that they took one look at my cheerleading uniform and decided that I must be vapid. Instead of shutting down, I was consistently kind and showed an interest in their lives. They warmed up gradually but not fully. I suppose the real punishment for being so harshly judgmental is that they missed out on the chance to be friends with me. As far as I'm concerned, the loss was one-sided.

One of Tom's friends sat down with me when we first started dating only to express outrage that a lowly cheerleader and sorority girl like myself would wind up dating a "good Christian boy." To say that I was taken aback would be an understatement. I was an honors student who hadn't missed a Sunday at Mass since I'd moved to college, and the number of people I'd been sexually intimate with could still be counted on one hand. This might be higher than the recommended Christian number of zero, but I wasn't out there living a life of debauchery and sin. (And even if I were, there's something in the New Testament about not judging). Unfortunately, I convinced her to give me a chance. This wasn't unfortunate in the sense that I didn't deserve a chance to date my own boyfriend but in the sense that no one with the audacity to be so flagrantly judgmental was worthy of my asking for one in the first place.

"I'm sorry I judged you unfairly," she conceded at the end of the conversation.

"Don't worry about it," I said casually, "It happens." We left it there.

Perhaps God was preparing me for my life as a Jew. Plenty of Jews don't like the way that other Jews live and pray. It is tempting to convince those other Jews to accept you, to acknowledge that your Judaism is also deep and true and valuable. But this sort of mongering for respect comes at too high a cost. To earn their respect, you have to abandon the respect that you have for yourself. Winning over the minds of self-righteous strangers is never worth what we have to give up in return. When people refuse to see your worth—as a Jew or Christian or otherwise—they refuse to see *you*, and they refuse to see the image of God within you. It's not your job to offer them a second look.

The ingroup/outgroup mentality requires a lot of cognitive dissonance. Theoretically, everyone is a sinner and is loved by Jesus; in practice, people not showing up to church and ranting about Jesus all the time are suspect. The implication is that non-churchgoers must be into sex, drugs, and general mayhem. There are plenty of churchgoing people into those very same activities, so you can see how the hypocrisy might grate. We allegedly believed that no one should have sex before marriage, but we were being sexually intimate before our one-year anniversary. I have no doubt that our church was avidly pro-life, but Tom was insistent that we get an abortion when my period was late once (though we weren't pregnant at all). I allegedly believed that Christians were obligated to spread the good word, but I had zero intention of being the person to bring up Jesus around a non-Christian. Thinking and doing were different concepts.

It wasn't hypocrisy that doomed our relationship. Tom never told me what to do, bless him, and we tried to save the Bible talk for actual Bible studies. From my perspective, the thing that did us in was mutual insecurity. For much of our senior year of college, I sensed that when things were going especially well for me, academically or otherwise, Tom bristled a bit. He didn't seem to like me outperforming him in a psychology class that we took together, and he was almost too gleeful to tutor me when I signed up to take music lessons, an area in which he unquestionably excelled. Everything felt like a strange competition. I would get panicky when Tom had plans that didn't involve me. I grew clingy, fearing that I couldn't be without him for an evening or two. I wondered if I was "too much" to be a good Christian wife. Too loud, too ambitious, too curious.

Our penetrative sex was painful for me but I found that I was too shy to articulate ideas about what would make it better. (It turns out that it was vaginismus and a need for different foreplay, and both of those issues are pretty easy to solve once the need is voiced). After a couple failed attempts at communication, I resorted to chatting and fantasizing with other men online behind his back. This was a mistake, both because online relationships can be dangerous and I made no effort to protect my privacy and also because it was dishonest and unkind. When Tom found out, I don't think he was able to recover his trust and confidence in our partnership. Though trust issues are common in situations like this, the pressure on men in our church to be leaders in their "homes" and on women to be meek and pious made it seem like our problem was a sign of fundamental brokenness that could be cured only by more religious devotion.

I told Tom that we could break up. He declined. But he occasionally went through my phone without telling me and reacted sensitively when other men showed me attention. When a stranger smiled at me at the gym one day, he demanded to know what I did to invite the attention. He snapped at me publicly when I got a text from an unknown number. It was a classmate in one of my Arabic classes, writing me to catch up. I told myself that I deserved it and that we had to make it work. In my mind, it would be better if we stayed together and got married "on time" like good Christians do.

Things shifted after graduation when Tom started to show small signs of aggression by raising his voice at me, once raising a fist and once throwing my keys at me while passersby gawked. Tom blamed his outbursts on the stress of looking for a job and trying to manage the behavior of his unruly new cat. Things never necessarily felt unsafe, but it was humiliating. I don't think it was his intention to harm me; in fact, even when he raised his fist, I knew in my heart of hearts that he wouldn't actually hit me. I think that Tom feared that if he wasn't in control, things would fall apart. That is, after all, how our pastors at Rock Band Church interpreted the Bible. Women don't lead; they follow. Eve's judgement is not to be trusted; Adam's is sound.

I mostly stopped going to church after graduation. I barely recognized myself, and I needed space from my ultra-Christian echo chamber to figure out where things had gone astray. I kept coming back to the idea of performance. I often had the sense that Tom was saying things that he had heard in church but didn't really mean. On our first date, he told me that he was looking for someone who could cook. This is unsurprising, since pastors frequently slipped tidbits about their wives' cooking and cleaning into their sermons.

"I make, like, pasta and frozen chicken breasts," I explained, whipping up some rotini pasta with olive oil and thyme, "It doesn't take any special skill."

"This pasta is so good, though," he gushed appreciatively.

"I really feel like you could do this," I teased, but I continued to cook, anyway. His helplessness seemed cute and made me feel important. To *serve*, supposedly, is to be like Jesus, and women serve by doing things like de-thawing chicken breast.

When talking about our future hypothetical children, Tom once remarked, "If we had two children, I'd feel like I was raising three." He had absolutely no reason to feel this way. I was competent enough for a 21-year-old. I cooked. I paid credit card bills on time. I was punctual. The need to infantilize adult women in order to justify their marginalization in a marriage and in the church was pervasive.

I also said things that I didn't believe. I told Tom that if he converted to Buddhism (a short-lived hypothetical suggestion) or stopped being "a believer," I'd have to break up with him rather than turn my back on Jesus. It was something I'd heard from women in my Bible study: we cannot marry non-believers; we must marry God-fearing men. My harsh words probably caused Tom to bury his seed of doubt when what he needed was to water it and see where it took him.

I felt like I was performing, too. Performing the role of a girlfriend who was willing to hide tampons in order to be modest, who didn't have new and evolving ideas about sex, who pretended that the word *service* didn't make me want to throw up. I was hard on Tom about his mistakes, taking them as a sign of some deep sinful nature rather than his being a human being. We weren't "broken" and in need of Jesus like our church droned on about, we were young and in need of some time to sort it all out.

That summer, I prepared my law school applications and moved into an apartment with my best friend Lizzie. I knew that Tom and I needed to end things, but I clung on to our relationship like a spiritual life vest. While Tom was battling feelings of worthlessness due to his inability to secure post-graduation employment, I was battling with my own source of shame: my growing feelings for my friend Rose. When Tom and I were on a negotiated break from dating, I posted a tasteful profile on CatholicMatch. com and then completely ignored it while I started seeing Rose instead. I told everyone, even Lizzie, that Rose was just a friend.

Homosexuality felt like the sin to end all sins at Rock Band Church. I'm not sure what made queer love such an easy target other than a bad translation of Leviticus, but I was petrified about what would happen to me if anyone found out. I wondered if I would lose friends or if there would be dramatic interventions. Moving off campus gave me more privacy than I'd ever had before, so I decided that the Shannon who occasionally went to Rock Band Church and the Shannon who invited Rose over when church was over were two different people. I convinced myself that dating Rose didn't really "count" because she also had a boyfriend (with whom she had an open relationship) so neither of us could possibly be anything other than straight. As long as I planned to get back together with Tom eventually, I was still a good heterosexual Christian.

Our dynamic had plenty of its own issues, but Rose was strides ahead of me in the self-acceptance department. I wasn't ready to be out as a queer or bisexual woman, so I didn't introduce Rose to anybody and panicked when she touched me in public. I could tell that my flightiness made her feel impatient and rejected. When I told her that we were "pretending to be lesbians" on a vacation in Saugatuck, Michigan, she gave me an incredulous look and asked what I thought I was doing. I told her I had no idea, and that was the truth.

Instead of, say, going to therapy and asking hard questions about what I wanted from my life and the relationships in them, I shut down and spent the summer working from 6am to 6pm at my new job. I told myself I was trying to make a name for myself at the start-up that employed me, but I was mostly avoiding being alone with my thoughts. In a stroke of good luck, my boss was Jewish, so when he had time, I asked him questions about Judaism in the most casual way possible. It was just like Judaism to be there at the right times, offering itself to me patiently while I struggled.

I can't remember how my break with Tom turned into an actual breakup. We lived at the same apartment complex. So, I dropped off his sweaters, and we stopped making eye contact if we bumped into each other. I broke up with Rose, too, though for reasons other than internalized homophobia. I am generally a proponent of maintaining a friendship after romantic relationships end, but I think I needed a clean break in order to shift from the person I was after Rock Band Church to the person I was going to be in the future, whoever that was. I let both Tom and Rose go and vowed to focus on myself instead.

Lizzie also encouraged me to take a break from dating. I had just proudly deleted the dating apps on my phone and my CatholicMatch.com account when my now-husband invited me out for tapas at Aventura Ann Arbor.

"Should I wait longer to date again?" I asked my mother on the phone.

"No!" she practically shouted, "I like him. He's the most normal person you've ever wanted to date. Go."

"I guess you should go," Lizzie conceded, "It's just dinner."

I went. I was blown away by how interested Travis was in my career and my thoughts. He wasn't threatened by my intelligence. He was patient and non-judgmental about the post-college mess I found myself in. He vowed to wait for as long as I needed to get on my feet. At work, Travis fought passionately for LGBT community members, immigrants, unions, and low-income families. He was wishy-washy on institutional religion, but he was not wishy-washy on the empathy that he had for other people.

I'd had a rough summer, so I wanted to do things right this time around. I asked Travis to wait, and he did. We came back together when the time was right and we've been sprinting toward the future together ever since.

Travis won me over with his steady patience and his deep respect for me. I knew that I was still growing—we all are— but that Travis would be there to support whoever I became. I once offered to take him to Rock Band Church. He refused.

"Sounds like a cult," he announced over his gin and tonic. "I don't do cults."

"That's unfair," I tried to tell him. "Cults are a serious business and a lot nastier than Rock Band Church. I just want to show you what it's like."

"Shoe fits," he said, sticking a fork into our shared risotto. "I'm not doing it." I gave up and never returned there, not with him and not by myself.

In every ending, there is a lesson. Rock Band Church taught me something important, which was that the death-and-resurrection of Jesus story didn't actually add up for me. Seeing myself as a broken sinner saved only by a human sacrifice started to strike me as uncomfortable rather than joyful. I rejected the stifling gender roles that Rock Band Church insisted on, and I doubted that "love the sinner, hate the sin" was actually a form of love at all when applied to things as fundamental as sexuality.

The performance of Christianity in the form of community service and Mass hadn't worked for me for a while, but when the theology piece started to break down, I decided to give Judaism a more serious look. I needed a place where every part of me would be nourished, a place where I could be loud and ambitious and curious and queer and uncertain without anyone needing to fix me. Judaism would eventually become the place where every part of myself could coexist in peace. I just needed to iron out some family details first.

CHAPTER 6

"Being deeply loved by someone gives you
strength, while loving someone deeply gives you
courage." *–Lao Tzu*

I didn't convert for marriage, but I think my husband's
soul was meant to convert with mine. The day that I met
Travis, I was 16 years old and had just been elected all-
school treasurer of our public high school. I was wearing
khakis and a white short-sleeved blouse from Hollister
to look "professional," and my hair—which my Conair
straightener pulverized every morning—laid totally flat
against my head. He was a year older than I and had been
elected school president. I never saw boys my age wearing
suits and ties, so I was enamored with his sharp outfit.
He had choppy, light brown hair and nerdy glasses. He
reached out and shook my hand. I decided on the spot that
I was in love with him.

Alas, Travis had a girlfriend already, so I spent the
rest of high school being hopelessly in love with him
(as in, the "crying while listening to Taylor Swift" kind
of love). Sometimes, I pretended that I needed a lift to

various student government events even though my mom offered repeatedly to drive me. I liked when he was driving me around in his old Saab. I didn't care that the car was older than we were; I was impressed that he could drive a stick shift. I told him that I had feelings for him on one of our drives, in the parking lot of a Taco Bell. Neither of us ordered food because both sets of our parents didn't approve of processed foods. We sat in the parking lot under the harsh light of the street lamps, he gripping the wheel tensely and I looking down at my hands. He rejected me very politely. For better or worse, love would have to wait.

We both attended the University of Michigan but stayed in our own bubbles; he in politics and I in Greek Life and athletics. It wasn't until after we'd both graduated from college and settled into our jobs that the stars would align. We were still in Ann Arbor long after our classmates had scattered around the country to find work in larger cities. Happy to remain in our cozy, liberal corner of Michigan for a while longer, we were able to hit our stride.

Once he and I had our real first date at Aventura, we were inseparable. On what was technically our third date, tipsy on Chop House martinis, we booked flights to New Orleans for the New Year.

"Are you seriously flying to Louisiana with someone you've gone on three dates with?" my roommate Lizzie asked skeptically. "Is that safe?"

"We went to high school together," I told her. "I promise he's okay."

"This is bold," she said, "But you go, girl. Keep me posted."

I promised I would.

The trip was amazing. On New Year's Eve, we went to the city's outdoor jazz concert and kissed under the fireworks while I shivered in the crisp December air. We ate at fancy seafood restaurants and shared our first beignet at Café Du Monde by moonlight. He had no idea that one day I would be committing us both to a shellfish-free life after we became Jewish and started keeping a kosher diet. Life is funny like that. When Travis dropped me off at my apartment after the trip, he teared up in the parking lot because he didn't want to say goodbye.

"I think I want to date him," I told Lizzie dreamily, laying on the floor in my new I Love New Orleans sweatshirt.

"Has it been enough time?" she asked.

"I'm going to look for engagement rings soon," I told her.

"You are out of control," she replied.

But I wasn't really kidding. My soul knew that I was supposed to marry Travis like my soul knew that it was supposed to become Jewish.

Travis and I didn't spend another night apart that year. We took turns staying over at each other's houses. He was terribly allergic to my roommate's cat, and he hated the creaky old bed that had been in my family for generations. It shook and rattled trying to accommodate the weight of both of us. The cat hated his guts and spent the night scratching his feet and flinging his car keys around to prove it.

"Are we a couple?" Travis asked one day, lying on top of me on his carpet and planting a kiss on my lips.

"You haven't asked," I pointed out.

"That seems a little old-fashioned," he said.

"I'd say yes," I promised him.

"Fine, will you be my girlfriend?" he asked, looking amused and adorably nervous. I said yes.

Travis loved to cook. He taught me how to make delectable seafood, flavorful stir fries, and vegetables that were actually edible. He liked taking me on dates to Ann Arbor's historic theaters or the museums in Detroit. He bought me flowers at all of the right times and let me watch *Dance Moms* to my heart's content even though he repeatedly reminded me that he didn't get the appeal. Travis would do anything for me, including converting to Judaism.

When we started dating, Travis wasn't Catholic. He was turned off by the church's refusal to perform same-sex marriages and told me that Catholic leadership meddled in politics too much. Travis grew up bouncing around churches of a few different denominations, but his parents were never sold on any particular religious doctrine. My in-laws are open-minded people, and my mother-in-law dismisses most churches as being "Kool-Aid places." My in-laws are a riot to hang out with. I don't blame them for being largely agnostic. I love them the way they are. Travis's Christian friends took him to various churches during his time in college, but he described never feeling a sense of belonging. He settled on an Episcopal church with a female pastor he admired. He described the church as welcoming "with the right amount of pomp and mystery," but he didn't seem committed. He agreed to attend St. Mary's with me until we found a more permanent spiritual home. I think his soul was waiting for Judaism, too.

St. Mary's was located in the building directly to the left of our studio apartment complex, so he chalked it up to convenience. I think he enjoyed attending St. Mary's the same way that I had as an undergraduate. We both admired the thoughtfulness of the Jesuits who ran the church, and Mass was a nice break from watching Bones and ordering pizza. Travis was passionate about supporting immigrants and caring for those in poverty, which were strengths of Catholic doctrine and practice. We were both passionately opposed to the death penalty and in favor of protecting natural resources. On both of these issues, the Catholic Church tends to be a leader in pushing for reform. There was plenty to disagree on, but we had enough to keep us coming back.

We enjoyed attending Mass when we were traveling, not because we were the type of Catholics who thought that skipping a week was a mortal sin but because Catholic churches in large American and European cities tend to be gorgeous. When we took our first international trip together, we attended Mass at Saint Mark's Basilica in Venice. We were the youngest in attendance by a few decades, but the nice thing about Roman Catholicism is that you can attend a service in almost any area of the world and know generally what's going on, whether you speak the local language or not. The same, of course, is true of Jewish services. It's nice to feel at home when you're not physically at home.

It wasn't Travis who pulled me away from the Church. I was ultimately the cause of the split, though not all at once. Somehow, once again, community service ended up being to blame for my woes.

Given how hectic my college years were, the transition to law school felt eerily calm. Travis was fairly busy with his political job during the week, but I found law school to be somewhat slow. I breezed through my reading assignments and spent the rest of the day texting Travis about when he was coming home so that I'd have company.

"Maybe you can find something fun to do after class," he urged politely. "You always said that you wanted to try fencing. Let's get you signed up." I took the hint and capitulated. I joined the University's fencing team and also signed up to help with jail ministry on weekends. Fencing was a great deal of fun; jail ministry was not. It was the single worst volunteer experience of my adult life.

Jail ministry involved showing up at the county prison with communion wafers for either the men or women because we couldn't perform a mixed-gender Mass; apparently there wasn't time to do two short services. When the women weren't up for Mass, my fellow volunteers and I would be sent into a spare room to sit around on hard plastic chairs and engage them in prayer. Usually, an older volunteer gave a talk about something that Jesus had helped him overcome while the women listened politely from their seats. I was painfully aware of the uncomfortable dynamic. Most of the women who attended services had been victims of abuse, addiction, or poverty. They didn't want to hear a 60-year-old white Catholic male drone on about the one time that his wife threatened to leave him and how Jesus pulled him through. It was never a two-way discussion. The volunteer would talk at them, his volume going up or down at unpredictable intervals, the women listening and occasionally nodding. By the time the impromptu sermon was over, we would stand in a circle and say a few communal prayers before it was time to go.

The first time I volunteered, I sat on a plastic chair with the other women and listened to the lead volunteer talk about how a picture of Jesus once fell off of his refrigerator when he was feeling down and he took it to be a sign from God that he shouldn't feel so sad. I gently kicked the metal leg of my chair with my heel in order to stay awake and took in the facial expressions of the other women. Each face was impassive, blank. This talk was boring and uninspiring. When it finally ended, a few women asked whether it would be possible for the priest to bring over the communion wafers after the Mass for the men was over.

"I don't know if we have enough wafers," the lead volunteer sighed, "If we have some left over, Catholic women can take communion first." Only one woman was Catholic. The others looked a little downtrodden.

"How very loving and inclusive," I whispered to a volunteer next to me.

"We're here for the Catholic women," she whispered back. How we were supposed to know which women were Catholic without interrogating them was unclear.

"They're stale, anyway, and they taste like moth balls," I whispered to a couple of the rejected women. They gave me small smiles back.

Only once did we get a block of free time in which we could engage one-on-one with the women. Spotting a woman who was sitting alone, I plopped down next to her.

"Are you doing okay?" I asked tentatively, "As okay as you can be under the circumstances?"

"No," she mumbled to the floor. "I'm not a Christian or anything, but I've been coming to these church things whenever we're allowed. I want to be a Christian. A lot of girls in here are. But I have to get my sexuality right with God. I had a boyfriend before this, and he was abusive. Since being here, I got a girlfriend. She treats me so much better. But I know that homosexuality isn't right." She folded her hands and continued to stare down at her lap.

"Whoever told you that was wrong," I said quietly, so that the other volunteers couldn't hear me. "What you have with your girlfriend sounds special. Don't let it go because some fool with a Bible told you that homosexuality is a sin. No God that I believe in would send you to hell for being in love. In fact, having to turn away from that love sounds like its own version of hell."

"I do love her," she said, looking more relaxed but still nervous.

"I'm not a priest, obviously," I told her, "but I don't think a homophobic interpretation of scripture is very credible coming from people who ignore the other 90% of Leviticus."

"Almost done here?" another volunteer asked suddenly, placing her chair between me and the woman I was speaking to.

"Not really," I answered.

"Well, we have to go," she announced, "And by the way, you're not supposed to talk to them about *that kind of stuff*." She gave me a pointed stare and turned to leave.

With that, someone opened the door, and we filed out of the room. My face felt hot, and my jaw was clenched tightly. I headed straight for the parking lot without a word to any of my fellow volunteers. This ministry, which was allegedly supposed to bring inmates closer to heaven, was its own special sort of hell. Boring, homophobic hell. I hopped into my car to head home and never went back.

I was shaken up by my experience with jail ministry, but we had already signed up for Catholic wedding prep, so the train needed to stay on the tracks for a while longer. Since Catholic priests aren't allowed to marry, we were assigned to do pre-marriage counseling with a deacon. (I was shocked when I learned that rabbis almost all had partners and children). Deacons are married, and ours had raised nine children, a combination of biological and adopted kids. Not every church assigns a married clergy member to counsel married couples, so we considered ourselves lucky. The deacon might have been old-fashioned, but he was a nice man. Our 5-hour-long sessions with him passed without incident. When the deacon balked at my plan to send our future kids to daycare, Travis jumped in with an air of finality and affirmed that we could manage our own careers, thank you very much. The deacon was sensible enough to let the issue go.

We also had to attend a weekend marriage seminar that mostly involved talking to already-married Catholic couples about topics of secular concern, like finances and in-laws. Travis seethed about the "natural family planning" session for a day or two, but I reminded him that no one was going to be spying on us in the bedroom. We tossed the "natural family planning" pamphlet in the recycling bin and replenished our condom supply. Having completed the steps necessary to be married in the Catholic Church, we were deemed hereby fit to become a nice Catholic family.

On the day of our wedding rehearsal, the priest went over the promises that we were to make to the Catholic Church on the day of our wedding. The sanctuary was empty other than my friends and family, standing lazily around and paying partial attention to the plans for the next day. Most of us had dressed up even though there was no one but the priest to see us. One of my friends wore sweatpants and Ugg boots in order to demonstrate her utter disdain for institutional religion. I ignored the gesture. The alter was dark and devoid of flowers but still smelled like Catholic churches often do: like a flower shop meeting incense. Travis and I held hands and gave our attention to the priest.

"Will you be faithful to one another?" the priest asked.

"We will," we echoed.

"Will you accept children lovingly from the Lord?" the priest asked us.

"Yes," we answered. Sure, we wanted them someday.

"Will you raise them in the ways of the Church?" he continued. We paused.

This felt like a large promise to make about the distant possibility of having a child. I was two weeks out from law school graduation, and we hadn't really set a timeline for bringing a baby into our world. I hadn't, until that day, thought of the fact that Catholic parents generally raise their children to be Catholic. I paused for a moment, standing on the altar in my sparkling white rehearsal dinner dress, and contemplated the weight of that.

It seems reasonable enough on the surface, but what a steep price to ask of two people who want a priest to officiate their wedding! Would I baptize my children? I pictured dressing them in a white gown and watching a priest sprinkle water over their heads to mark them free of original sin, a theory that I thought was cruddy and untrue. Did I want to baptize my children before they had a chance to choose the Christian path for themselves? Would I expect them to attend Mass every Sunday? What about Sunday school? What if any of my children had questions about female leadership or wanted to marry someone of the same sex? I felt suddenly overwhelmed.

With everyone staring expectantly at us, Travis and I nodded and recited what we were supposed to. It wasn't until I was outside in the cold December air that I felt like I could breathe again.

I woke up the next day to unbelievably good weather. It was sunny and over 40 degrees in early December. The sun was rising as my friends and I pulled up to Zingerman's Cornman Farms, where we would be getting dressed before heading to the church. It was a really beautiful day. We got ready, fiddling with the ribbon on my dress and chatting until it was time to go to the church. In the basement of the church, my mom pinned my long, flowing veil on my head, and my dad took my arm, ready to walk me down the aisle.

We opted for the full hour-long wedding Mass, much to the chagrin of our friends and family. If you're going to do the thing, do it right, I suppose. During our wedding Mass, the priest gave a homily that didn't mention either of us; in fact, it was a metaphor about wine that involved telling our gathered loved ones to find hope in the Lord even when we feel like squashed grapes. "Squashed grapes" became quite the joke among our friends in the following weeks. Nonetheless, the music was lovely, and when Travis kissed me at the end of the service, everyone clapped. We smiled and smiled, all the way back down the aisle and out into the crisp winter air.

We eventually did a full Jewish wedding under a *chuppah* [a Jewish wedding canopy], but without all of the guests or the tiered wedding cake. Rabbi Rubenstein's sermon at our wedding was significantly more touching. I don't, however, feel upset about the fact that our first wedding wasn't Jewish. Things tend to happen at the right time even if the wait is painful.

CHAPTER 7

Family is where you're meant to be most free.
–*Michele Meleen*

Our wedding day was gorgeous, but it made one thing abundantly clear: my family was not very invested in being Catholic. Most of our family members declined to take communion on our wedding day, and nearly everyone whined to me about the length of the Mass. If I had been staying Catholic for the sake of family unity, it was an exercise in futility. My mom is a complicated woman: she did not much like Catholicism, but she didn't want me to leave it for Judaism.

"I'm positive that my parents only went through with the Catholicism thing because of my birth mother," I told Travis the morning after our wedding, curling up in the passenger seat of our Impala. "Planning that wedding Mass was nothing but grief."

"It doesn't matter, babe," he smiled, kissing my hand as we merged onto the highway, "We're married."

"Yeah, we are," I whispered back. He was right. We were married, and the stress of planning a wedding was behind us. Why dwell on it?

I had never been particularly curious about my birth parents. This is hard for people to digest, especially other adoptees who have invested significant resources in tracking down their biological families. I was, at best, intermittently and passively curious about my origins. At moments during my childhood, it would suddenly reoccur to me that I had been adopted, for example, when someone told me that I had my adoptive mother's eyes. I so rarely thought about the adoption that I always found myself surprised to remember that my mother hadn't given birth to me. Like many adoptions, mine was prearranged by social workers when my birth mother faced an unplanned pregnancy. My parents picked me up from the hospital a few days after I entered the world. They were always my parents, as far as I was concerned. Adoption, to me, was a theoretical concept.

My adoptive family was more than enough for me. I had a small, tight-knit group of relatives. No one yelled; no one drank. My mother said yes to everything I wanted. My parents never missed a gymnastics competition, and they sold Girl Scout cookies like their lives depended on it. My maternal grandmother was the light of my life, and my paternal aunt was the funniest person I knew. I had terrifically fun cousins who took me camping every summer and taught me how to swear. Our neighbor, a close friend of my mom's, let me march into her house at will to raid the cookie jar. In my little world, I didn't need anyone else.

"My birth mother wasn't ready for a baby, was she?" I asked my grandmother one day during one of our weekend sleepovers. I was probably between ten and twelve. I don't know what made me think of it.

"No," my grandmother confirmed, gently fingering a baby photo of me on her wall. I was wearing a red velvet dress with a large white bow and smirking shyly at the camera. "But look what I got," she added, smiling at me and putting her hand on my head.

"Can we make a banana split now?" I asked, turning away from my baby photo with a satisfied shrug. There wasn't anything else I needed to know. We didn't discuss it again.

I never felt bitter about the adoption. I never felt anything. Unlike Travis, who loves ancestry projects, I grew up making do with what I knew about my parents' families. My dad's family is Polish, so I decided that I was Polish, too. I liked pierogis, so why not? My grandmother was a tough Irish woman, so I liked to think that I was Irish, too. This was how I proceeded for 25 years of my life.

When I suggested that Travis and I order 23&Me kits to confirm that we weren't secretly related before we reproduced, he was taken aback. I had never cared about my ancestry before, and I didn't really care about it then. But I needed to know that we didn't have a long-lost-cousin situation on our hands, so he agreed. We spit in the little plastic tubes and mailed them off. I didn't wait around anxiously for the results. I went about my life and more or less forgot that I was waiting on them to come back at all.

The results were ready when we were visiting family and friends in Portland. We were staying with one of my aunts and two younger cousins. They were all sleeping in when I got the email first thing in the morning the day after we had arrived. I logged into my account, rubbing my eyes absentmindedly. The first thing I did was connect my account to Travis's.

"We share 0% DNA!" I told him with a grin.

"I knew we didn't share DNA," he said with an eye roll, more interested in peeling his banana than discovering the wonders of his own genetic profile.

"You didn't know that," I insisted, "You don't watch enough reality TV."

"You watch too much," he countered without looking up from his breakfast.

I start to click through the rest of the data. I ended up being Irish, like my grandmother. I was not Polish, to my slight disappointment, but Lithuanian. I open a new tab on my laptop so that I would remember to look up facts about Lithuanian food and culture later.

"I'm a teeny tiny bit Ashkenazi," I told Travis. "My earliest ancestors seemingly came from Cyprus." I clicked through the colorful charts with glee. The data correctly guessed my hair texture and eye color. It even made predictions about the texture of my ear wax and presence of stretch marks. It was more fun than I had anticipated.

And then the fun was over.

"*Urgh!*" I exclaimed, splashing hot coffee on my thigh. "Oh, no! Oh, no! This is not good. It *found her.*"

"Found who?" Travis asked, though he must have suspected who it was.

"My birth mother," I hissed back. "Karen." His jaw dropped open. I'm sure he couldn't have formed words if he tried.

I clicked on her profile, but there was nothing particularly illuminating to see. I could see that Karen was heavily Italian, a bit Iberian. She didn't seem to have any other close DNA matches in the system. There was her name, though, and the fact that we shared over 49% of our DNA. My hands were shaking. I slammed my computer shut and stepped outside. It was cool and damp in the Pacific Northwest, but I barely felt the cold on my uncovered arms. Travis followed me outside and stuffed his hands in his pockets.

"What are you going to do?" he asked.

In response, I shouted a curse word to the treetops. I felt more dread than excitement. Finding one's birth parents is a very big decision, and when the decision is made for you, it doesn't feel like a "miracle" so much as it feels like an intrusion. I did not want to spend our vacation with this heaviness hanging over me. I cursed to the treetops again for good measure. Travis got the message and went back inside to retrieve my caffeine.

Within hours, I started getting more emails from 23&Me, informing me of other DNA matches. It quickly became clear that Karen would be notified of my existence, especially given the closeness of the genetic relationship. I wondered if there was a way to turn the notifications off. There had to be some sort of privacy setting that would protect my newfound discovery for a few days. I was unfamiliar with the website, and my hands were shaking too badly to figure it out.

It was time for game theory: do I make the first move, or do I let her come to me? If I didn't reach out, Karen might assume that I hadn't seen her name at all. More realistically, she would know that I got the same email that she received notifying her of the match. To ignore the email and not reach out to her seemed remarkably ungrateful. What kind of cold-hearted offspring ignores that sort of elephant in the room?

On the other hand, Karen had chosen a closed adoption. She hadn't even written a letter or left me with a trinket. She wanted no contact, and who was I to intrude on her personal life now? It felt impossible to decide. I plopped down on the wet sidewalk and implored myself not to vomit. Travis stood there awkwardly, mug in his hands, wondering what to say.

A day later, we connected, politely and tentatively. It doesn't matter who initiated. Nothing in our early conversations went horribly wrong, but something felt undeniably off, like a lid had been pried off of a private part of my life and wouldn't go back on. The entire vacation was ruined by my constant anxiety and preoccupation with the new discovery. I don't know if I ever felt *happy*. It was more a haze of disbelief, a nagging sense of unreality that followed me around and prohibited me from enjoying the sights and sounds that Portland had to offer. My conversations with my birth mother were benign: our favorite classes in law school (she was also a lawyer, by chance), our respective family members, favorite sports, personality traits. Karen was charming and clearly self-assured. She was a spiritual person. Still Catholic. She lived in a major city on the East Coast and had no other children. My biological father and she hadn't spoken in years, but she offered to connect us.

The reunion was met with awe from our friends and family. People cannot imagine going an entire lifetime without knowing where they came from, so to them, finding one's birth parents is a fantastic development. I cannot tell you how many acquaintances marveled over the "wonders of the universe" that brought us together. I politely agreed with them and changed the topic. I did not necessarily think that this was all fantastic. I suspected that the universe didn't have a "plan," or at least not a very good one. I didn't see the romance in the situation the way that other people seemed to.

For the most part, my birth parents and I exchanged information about ourselves and our interests. We had some things in common and not others, i.e., we were like any other strangers that exist on God's green earth. Anyone can find common ground with anyone, and no one is exactly alike, genetics notwithstanding. I did not make much of whether we all like the same music (we don't), or vote the same way (I vote like my bio father). Karen was disappointed that I didn't share her love for Italian-American cuisine, but my birth father was tickled that we both enjoyed Good Humor ice cream bars. My birth father told me that he is an atheist.

I was somewhat happy to have an answer to the question of who created me even if it's not a question I had ever dwelled on. But turns out that a 25-year absence made the reunion awkward and difficult. I could have predicted that. I never fell for fairy tale "finding the birth parent" stories, and I was right to be skeptical. My biological father was calm and had no expectations. We got along swimmingly and still do. I love that guy.

Things fell apart slowly and a touch dramatically with Karen. We do not keep in contact. She was a logical person and I don't think her unkind. She had a tendency, however, to say things that were inappropriate and was too stubborn to walk them back. I was stubborn like that as a child, but I grew into an adult who is comfortable being wrong. Talking to her was often like talking to the sixth-grade version of myself: painful and fruitless.

Some of her more controversial comments included "Most millennials are dumpster-diving vegans" and "There is no such thing as false felony convictions in the criminal justice system." I mostly ignored these off-the-wall political views. It was the things she said about *me* that tanked our relationship.

"Anything I don't like about you, you got from your father," Karen told me one day.

"That's not how genetics work," I responded, wounded. "I'm a full person, not divisible into genetic parts. You don't get to take credit for anything good about me, and it's not his fault that I also have flaws."

"I'm taking credit for the good," Karen said firmly. I tried to tease out whether she was joking. To take credit for my success after a 25-year absence was a bad joke, but it became downright offensive when I realized that she was serious.

"What's wrong with her?" Travis asked when I told him about the conversation.

"I'll talk to my therapist about it," I assured him. "She's happy that I'm doing well, and she's trying to take credit for it."

"That doesn't excuse it," he argued.

"I know," I said. "We'll work it out."

On another day, she texted me out of the blue about my sewing skills.

"I can't really sew," I texted her, "Not by hand. A little bit with a machine."

"I knew it," Karen typed back, "Because you're a spoiled millennial." I stopped in my tracks and stared at my phone in disbelief. I wasn't sure what had set her off about my response, and to be honest, I wasn't very interested in finding out.

"What the hell," Travis snapped when he read the exchange.

"I don't know," I grumbled, "She has this whole doomsday fear. Zombie apocalypse or whatever. She thinks everyone should know how to take care of themselves."

"It's not okay," he insisted again.

"She's different," I tried to explain. "She's experienced a lot of trauma. I ordered a sewing kit just in case."

"We don't need a sewing kit," he snapped.

"I'm over it," I lied. I abandoned my phone and went to my apartment's gym. I ran on the elliptical for almost an hour, until my glowing rage had burned down to a nub of annoyance. I convinced myself that these were normal growing pains.

Karen and I continued to text even though I knew things were becoming toxic. We were like flies to the proverbial lightbulb.

"My dad called me to remind me that I'm your parent and not your friend," she texted me a week or so later.

"Your dad is wrong. You're not my parent," I explained, as gently as possible. "I have parents. I'm about to become a parent myself. I am not in the market for parental guidance."

"I am your parent," she repeated stubbornly. True to form, she began trying to tell me what to do. She threw a small fit that I had no plans to invite her to my swearing-in ceremony as an attorney. She tried to forbid me to get a small tattoo on my rib cage. I patiently explained that she could not, and did not, occupy that role in my life. She fought back. Travis seethed on my behalf. I got the tattoo and was sworn in with only my mother, husband, and mother-in-law in attendance.

My therapist suggested that text messaging is difficult to navigate and that while I shouldn't rush an in-person meeting, perhaps it would be helpful to have more verbal conversations in lieu of email and text. I agreed. I invited Karen to meet with me at the University of Michigan, the very place where she had given birth. This turned out to be a shortsighted move.

During her visit, Karen didn't seem terribly emotional. We had tea together and ate dinner with my mother. Things were a little awkward, but there were no explosions. At one point, she suggested a walk around campus.

"No, thanks," I told her, stirring my chamomile tea and squirming uncomfortably in my chair, "I'm very familiar with it."

That isn't why I decided not to tour campus with her. It was because she talked about the pregnancy all the time and it made me uneasy. Karen did not fret over her decision to put me up for adoption, but she made it clear that it was no joy to be a pregnant woman on campus. She lost one of her jobs and struggled to afford healthy food options. I sympathized, but what was I supposed to say about a tumultuous time in her life that I had no memory of? At this point, I had never been pregnant and couldn't relate to the symptoms.

"You were a tyrant," Karen told me, "I was always throwing up, and I failed my classes that term."

"Lots of people get morning sickness," I offered weakly.

"I have a hard time with you having opinions now," she said. "You never did in the womb."

"I understand that it's different, me being sentient now," I replied uneasily.

I couldn't stomach walking around campus with her incessantly dumping the emotional baggage of an unplanned pregnancy on me. Maybe that's unfair. Maybe I should have tried harder. In the end, we went out for dessert, instead. The next day, we attended Mass together—Karen, Travis, and me. My real mother did not come. Karen returned to the airport after that, and I had a chance to process the visit.

"It went pretty well," I told Travis as she drove off.

"I guess so," he said skeptically, not knowing what to make of the whole ordeal.

Days after she returned home, we had another fight.

"You're so selfish," Karen said, "You never once thought about how meaningful it would be for me to walk around campus with you. The campus where I carried you internally. You don't think about other people."

I understood why she felt that way, but I refrained from apologizing. I had my reasons, and they were valid. Anyone who knows me will tell you that I do, in fact, think about other people. I also respect my own boundaries. I haven't struck a perfect balance between the two—I don't think anyone does—but I wasn't going to let someone who had just met me tell me what a selfish person I was. Her insults didn't sting anymore; it felt like she was describing someone she didn't know.

That's because she was.

Karen thought maybe another meeting would help. My therapist disagreed, but maybe I had one of those stubborn genes, after all. We tried to negotiate the details of a second meeting, but it ended in disaster. Karen wanted to plan the trip on her own as a "surprise."

I don't like surprises. She wouldn't tell me what we were going to do when we met in an unfamiliar city, so I threatened to pull out.

"I won't have you ruin this entire trip with your whining," she told me. I am many things, but I am certainly not a whiner. I was a grown woman with my own family, and she wanted to treat me like I was the child she never got to raise. I put my foot down swiftly.

"I know it's hard for you to digest my autonomy as an adult, but you don't have a choice. I'm not showing up in a different state without a clue as to what's happening," I insisted.

"It's not my fault your parents raised you to be such a control freak." I considered that an insult to the people who loved me and raised me when she could not. I still didn't feel bitter about the adoption, but the idea that she would speak negatively about my parents was enough to light a fire within me. I was enraged.

I backed out of the trip and typed her a long, firm email about boundaries. Travis offered to edit the email for me, but I declined. This was between Karen and me. I needed to talk to her on my own terms.

She did not receive it well. "Yeah. We're done here. I'd like to go back to a closed adoption," she wrote.

It was cruel but almost a relief. Her utter disregard for my feelings was the permission that I needed to let this whole thing go. I took a deep breath and filled my lungs with air. I closed my computer and left her email behind.

"Let's go for a jog," I told Travis, "I'm all set here."

Travis was terrified that I was concealing my hurt. He braced for a breakdown for weeks. My therapist agreed with him and pushed me to talk about how distraught I was. I assured them both that I had never felt freer. That wasn't a lie.

Finding my birth mother wasn't the gift that people had hoped for me, but there was a gift in the situation after all. This was the last reason that I needed to leave the Church behind. Catholicism had been handed down to me as some sort of pact between my young, religious birth mother and my barely Catholic parents. I was under no obligation to stay.

Catholicism had been forming small cracks over time. My Sunday school experience, mission trips, purity culture, and jail ministry were all little chinks in the armor of faith that turned me toward Judaism, but I never had the gumption to go through with the change. Until this.

It was not out of resentment or animus that this last fracture took hold. My biological mother had given me the gift of life and insisted upon a Catholic upbringing. My parents had fulfilled that mission faithfully, and now here I was, an unhappy Catholic, ready to start my own family. I felt that things had come full circle. Perhaps it was the universe telling me that I was allowed to move on. It had become a matter of when rather than if.

I was shaken by my experience with my birth mother and overwhelmed by the demands of my young marriage and budding legal career. I spent a lot of time in therapy working my way out of the woods. I teetered back and forth between staying Catholic or undergoing conversion during this fragile time period. It's almost like I was waiting for a sign, something other than my own foolhardy notion that I needed to be Jewish.

The sign came not half a year later, as two pink lines on a First Response test.

CHAPTER 8

"Pain is reality, suffering is a choice."
–Rabbi Asher Resnick

When Travis and I got pregnant with our first baby, we were regularly attending Old St. Patrick's Church in the West Loop of Chicago. After our wedding, I had buried myself in bar exam prep and transitioned directly into my new role as a bona fide lawyer. I was fencing at a local club for exercise, filling my limited spare time with trying every restaurant on Randolph Street. For a while, I largely forgot that I had considered leaving the Church. Our church was really an excellent place. Every Sunday, we made ourselves a nice vegetarian dinner, poured a glass of red wine, and ended the evening by going to the 9 p.m. Mass. In the dark and quiet of those late-night weekend Masses, I found a spark of spirituality that had felt dead for a long time. The Church was run by kind, sharp priests. The homilies tended to focus on social justice issues. The priests usually talked about issues of importance to the community— gun violence in Chicago, racism and segregation, care for the poor. The Church openly supported LGBTQ members and devoted resources to community projects, like a restorative justice program. In theory, it should have been the perfect place for me to maintain my Catholic identity. And for a while, so I did.

We found out we were pregnant the summer after I had my law school graduation and the wedding. We had been married for six months and couldn't wait any longer to add to our family. I should have been excited, but instead, I was a ball of nervous energy.

For reasons I can't explain, I was filled with a deep sense of foreboding. I begged Travis not to get his hopes up since there are no guarantees in early pregnancy. We did not plan a pregnancy announcement, nor did we talk about baby names. When I called my mom to tell her the news, I didn't exclaim that she was going to be a grandma. I called her from my car while battling traffic on Lakeshore Drive and offered a noncommittal, "We got pregnant, but we'll see how it goes." I was no longer in therapy, but everyone assured me that it was nothing more than my anxiety. A few people suggested meditation. I signed up for a couple of yoga classes and tried to pray the anxiety away.

I woke up every morning and anxiously assessed myself for any characteristic symptoms of pregnancy: nausea, sore breasts, fatigue. I took a pregnancy test twice a day to make sure that there really was a baby developing inside of me. Nothing I did shook the sense of fear that had overtaken me.

Some people describe being utterly shocked by a miscarriage. Some people don't even know of the possibility. For me, miscarrying felt like confirmation of a truth that had been buried deep inside of me since I saw the word "pregnant" on that digital test: the pregnancy wasn't going to last.

At this point in our marriage, Travis was living and working in Detroit as a summer associate, and so he was only in Chicago with me on weekends. Naturally, when the bleeding started, I was alone. I called my doctor's office with shaking hands, and they agreed to see me right away.

I was due in court within the hour, and neither of my supervisors knew I was pregnant yet. I left the supervisor I liked better a shaky voicemail and flew down Lakeshore Drive to my doctor's office. Despite knowing the likely outcome, I was so nervous that I abandoned my car in an illegal parking spot.

I fully expected for my doctor to tell me that I was having a miscarriage. Despite being mentally prepared for that outcome, I was not prepared for how angry and empty the diagnosis made me feel. It was so very infuriating to have gotten a positive pregnancy test but have to accept there would be no baby. As I stared at the ceiling, trying to calm myself down, my doctor explained that she couldn't see anything in my uterus. Unless my dates were off (they weren't), the pregnancy was either an ectopic pregnancy or a failed intrauterine pregnancy. Both of those outcomes are depressing, but one can be life-threatening. I waved my hand to indicate that I knew what an ectopic pregnancy was, lest my doctor try and explain. I was, after all, the queen of Googling all of the ways in which a pregnancy could go wrong. Not for the first time, I wished that my amassed knowledge was theoretical instead of practical.

"Were you trying to get pregnant?" my doctor asked neutrally.

"Yes!" I spat back indignantly. It was too painful to hear someone suggest that my much-desired pregnancy had been nothing more than an accident. Though, in truth, my doctor was right to be surprised. I had told her six months prior during a pap smear that we had no plans to get pregnant right away after our wedding. I'm not sure what changed our minds about trying to conceive sooner. It definitely had something to do with seeing a very cute baby in a puffy purple snowsuit during our Easter vacation to the United Kingdom. Travis and I took one look at the happy family and decided to fly back to America and get pregnant. I wish I were joking. Even if the decision was haphazardly made, there was no denying that I loved and wanted this child. To lose a wanted pregnancy feels utterly inhumane.

I took slow, steady breaths and kept my face impassive. I didn't know my doctor well enough to have an emotional breakdown in front of her, so I focused on the facts. I kept my voice calm and even. Get some blood drawn, follow up in two days, call in the event of sharp abdominal pain or excessive bleeding. The room felt empty without Travis there to take in the news with me. It was just my doctor, sitting calmly on her stool, and I. I wanted to hold Travis's hand, but since he was 300 miles away, I dug my fingers into the crunchy sterile paper beneath me and tried not to scream.

It occurred to me that I needed to tell Travis immediately. I scrambled for my phone in a panic. Dear God, what on earth was I going to tell my him? That his baby was gone before it had really had a chance to develop? That what I told him on the phone was probably "no big deal" was actually a "very big deal because the baby is gone"?

I started to type out a message to him before realizing that I wasn't yet alone. My doctor got up to leave. I kept my hands poised over Travis's name on the screen.

"It's important that you come back in 48 hours so that we can monitor your levels," she instructed.

I didn't look up. My emotional walls were starting to crumble. Tears began to cloud my vision. The room was closing in on me, and I felt like I was going to vomit.

"I need to know that you understand me," my doctor said. The door was already halfway open, and I could tell that she was growing impatient.

"Yes, whatever," I snapped. I bit my lip as hard as I could to stop myself from crying.

When my doctor stepped out of the room and the door clicked shut behind her, I curled up into a tiny ball underneath my thin, starchy sheet. I dialed Travis. Better to call than text. Hot tears were flowing down my cheeks at this point, but I could hear people milling around outside of the room so I spoke quickly and quietly.

"Baby," I choked out when he answered the phone, "There's nothing in my uterus. The baby didn't make it. I have to get dressed and go to work. But I'm so sorry."

Before he could respond, a nurse was already knocking on the door, eager to kick me out so that she could clean the room for the next patient.

I dried my tears and focused again on what I had to do: put on pants, walk to lab, offer arm for blood draw, walk to elevator, walk to car, drive to work.

Travis asked me what he should do. The pain that I could hear in his voice was unbearable. I tried to remember what day it was. He wasn't due to come back to Chicago until Friday evening. It was only one day, but it felt impossible.

"I'll take tomorrow off. I'll come home tonight. I'll let them know it's a family emergency." I could tell he was crying.

I quickly agreed. That meant I only had to be by myself for a handful of hours after work if I could somehow survive the workday.

I called my mom on the way to work to tell her the news. Hearing her voice kept me calm enough to drive to work. I didn't make it farther than that. I cried in the parking structure at my office for 30 minutes before texting my supervisor that I wasn't going to make it in after all.

I went home, changed into sweatpants, and hid under the covers. And in bed is where I stayed—for days—until the miscarriage began.

It happened over Independence Day weekend. After days of waiting and crying, I woke up to wicked cramping and a gush of blood. I asked Travis if we should try to contact a priest.

"What are we going to tell them?" Travis cringed. "We can't show up at a church on a holiday weekend with... blood and tissue."

He was right. I was not in any state to throw a funeral for my unborn child. The details of the conversation would be too grotesque to bear. Instead, I miscarried silently at home, curled up in the shower, taking slow, deep breaths, Travis pacing the hall in a sort of zombie state. I had only been six weeks pregnant, so as far as miscarriages go, it was over fairly quickly. By the same time the following week, there was no evidence that I had ever been pregnant at all.

We named the baby Vesper, Latin for *night star* or *night prayer*.

We wasted no time trying to conceive again. My miscarriage happened in early July, and by early October, we had another positive pregnancy test. I was nervous, but I had a bit more confidence in this pregnancy. The chances of having two consecutive miscarriages at 25 years of age were slim.

We were still going to Mass on Sunday evenings, but I had long stopped asking for God to help me get pregnant or stay pregnant. I would sit in my pew and focus on letting my mind go blank. I didn't think about my job. I didn't think about my pregnancy or about trying to conceive. It was an hour where I could enjoy silence, willing my heart to stop racing with the anxiety that plagued me all week, between law firm assignments and checking my underwear incessantly for blood. I pictured my anxious thoughts floating up and away, toward the lanterns hanging down from the ceiling like flickering teardrops. I wasn't going to church to talk to Jesus. I was going so that I didn't have to talk or think at all. There is sometimes no medicine as potent as stillness.

In a cruel twist of fate, our second pregnancy was neither obviously healthy nor obviously unhealthy. I started bleeding in miniscule amounts around 7 weeks. I spent multiple days each week in my doctor's office, fretting and crying over my tiny baby's growth (or lack thereof) and the on-again-off-again bleeding that could be totally harmless but could also be a sign of imminent miscarriage. I quickly moved on from my fear of crying in front of medical staff. I cried all the time. My doctor was consistently calm and practical. She never insulted me by sugarcoating things to spare my feelings. She treated me like I was strong and competent.

And most of the time, I was. The anxiety came in unpleasant waves. Instead of working when I was at my office, some days I Googled signs of miscarriage so much that I was sure that someone from IT would burst in to ask whether or not I planned to use the firm computer for legal research or not. I drove to my doctor's office for check-in ultrasounds so frequently that my GPS started pulling up the building when I got into my car to drive to the grocery store on weekends. I was tormented with the fragility and uncertainty of it all, but I tried to stay positive. On my best days, I would take a CTA bus to the East Bank Club and run gently on an elliptical in their cavernous cardio room, as if moving too quickly or aggressively might upset the baby. Most days, I survived by traveling between work and my bed and eating a concerning number of tortilla chips.

One weekend, I bled so much that I called my doctor's office and let them know that the pregnancy was over. When I arrived for my D&C procedure that Monday, I had cried every tear left in me. I was, as much as I could be, at peace with saying goodbye to another pregnancy. I laid back and opened my legs so that my doctor could confirm that the baby was no longer with us. She sounded almost apologetic when she gently informed me that the baby still had a heartbeat. So, we waited—a little hopeful, mostly terrified.

When the baby's heartbeat finally did stop, I had achieved an impressive, if not concerning, level of numbness. My doctor put her hand on my arm and told me she was sorry.

"It's fine," I said, the resoluteness in my voice surprising even me. "It's not your fault. It's all going to be okay."

I looked up at Travis. He looked sad, tired. We made eye contact and nodded at one another. There was pain, but there was also closure. Neither of us needed to say anything more.

When my doctor gently offered to schedule a D&C for the second time, I suddenly balked. The guilt that I was feeling took me by surprise.

"I don't know … if … if Catholics … *allow* a D&C," I mumbled, embarrassed by my instinct to defer to the doctrine of a Church that I had barely felt at home in for years.

"I think if there's no heartbeat …" my doctor began, but she didn't finish her thought. She looked as tired as I felt.

"I think it's something about the tissue. If we do the D&C, it's going to be thrown away in a lab. I think it has to be buried."

I had no idea what I was talking about, really, but I had the sense that I needed to do right by this baby, and I was desperately grasping at straws in an attempt to figure out what needed to be done next.

My doctor agreed that we had time to think about it. I could see that she was grieving for me, too. How difficult must it be to witness someone's pain in this way, in one of the most private and difficult moments of their lives, but be forced to maintain the right degree of care and professional distance.

I had dragged our parents, our medical staff, and my friends on this unpleasant emotional roller coaster with me, and they all stepped up to the plate when we needed them most. I was still in the habit of praying, of course, but I already had what—or whom—I needed to weather the storm. Maybe if there is a God up there sending us gifts, we don't have to look much farther than the people we're surrounded with.

In the end, I agreed to do the D&C.

We named this baby David, Hebrew for "beloved."

I took a bit of time off work to emotionally and physically recover. In order to pass the time between doses of Tylenol and Motrin, I found my way to the local synagogue's website and downloaded the Jews by Choice recommended reading list. When I couldn't focus on my work and couldn't relax enough to nap, I would open one of the books from the list and read a chapter or two. I started with Harold Kushner's *To Life*. Curled up in my sweatpants a few days after my D&C, I came to the following passage:

> Nature might be beautiful and orderly but it is morally blind. Falling rocks and speeding bullets obey laws of physics, irrespective of what harm they may do to innocent people in their path. The sages of the Talmud put it this way: If a man steals seeds and plants them, it would be morally fitting if the stolen seeds would refuse to grow. But the world of Nature follows its course, and the seeds grow.

These words were not necessarily heartwarming, but it was the first thing that had brought me genuine comfort in weeks. I was sick of wondering whether God had a plan, and whether my pain had any meaning. It was a tired cycle. Kushner's words were like a cool glass of water after a hike in the desert. Sperm met egg because Travis and I made it so, and sperm and egg did not divide and reproduce correctly because nature is what it is. Beautiful, frightful, unstoppable. We either spend our lives fighting with nature and denying its power, or we accept it and turn to religion for the comfort to cope with whatever nature throws at us. I didn't want to twist myself into a theological pretzel to prove that my unborn children were taken for a reason that I was too mortal to comprehend. It seemed to me that life could get murky just because that's how things are.

Judaism felt like permission to believe that. When I finished the book, I typed out an email to the local Jews by Choice program before I could change my mind. I wrote that I wanted to be Jewish, and I waited anxiously to hear back.

In the meantime, I was really starting to feel the Hanukkah spirit. I dragged Travis to Target to buy a menorah. We still hadn't had the conversion conversation, but he didn't ask questions when I informed him that we'd be lighting candles for Hanukkah, and this is why I love him. We had decided to take a break from trying to conceive so that we could reset and enjoy our marriage. We booked a trip to Boston for the New Year, and I threw myself back into my work with renewed energy.

We lit our Hanukkah candles every night and totally butchered the Hebrew prayers that go with them. It felt good to think about something other than pregnancy. I even picked up raspberry *sufganiyot* for my office, and sent a vague note that I had left "Hanukkah treats in the kitchen." I didn't correct the colleagues who emailed back to wish me a Happy Hanukkah.

When I returned to my obstetrician's office for the two-week post-op follow up, I came bearing a box of festive Hanukkah cookies from Big Fat Cookie, one of my favorite Chicago small businesses. I didn't tell my doctor that despite being Catholic before she operated on me, I was decidedly almost Jewish now. In fact, I still hadn't clued Travis in on that particular secret yet. I wished my doctor an enthusiastic Happy Hanukkah, and went home and frantically refreshed my email, hoping to hear from the Jews by Choice program director.

The cantor, of course, said that she was happy to have us lay a foundation for Judaism in her program. She offered us a chance to meet in her office to discuss the course, which I accepted on my own behalf with a promise that I'd speak to Travis. She ended her email with "Happy Hanukkah!"

For the first time in a long time, I was filled with warmth.

CHAPTER 9

"I long, as does every human being, to be at home
wherever I find myself." –*Maya Angelou*

A week after Travis and I had our riveting car
conversation about converting to Judaism, we took a New
Year's Eve trip to Boston. Our tradition of going away
for New Year's Eve started with our impromptu trip to
New Orleans years earlier, and it was a tradition that we
kept up. We love to travel when it's cold and crisp outside,
exploring new cities while bundled up and sipping hot
drinks. It's a nice chance to reset after the end-of-year
push to wrap up law firm projects and the days spent
cooped up with family at Christmas time. This year we
were especially looking forward to leaving the ovulation
tests and prenatal gummies behind.

While looking up sights to explore in Boston, I got
the brilliant idea for us to visit a synagogue. Even better:
we should attend services at a synagogue. It would have
been sensible if our first official trip to a synagogue took
place as part of our conversion course. If I had waited a
few weeks, I could have taken a nice low-stakes field trip

to Anshe Emet's sanctuary with the guidance of my fellow converts. Always one to jump the gun, I decided that there was no time like the present.

I still had not told a soul besides Travis that we were beginning the conversion process, so I was on my own to figure out which synagogue to visit. During the flight, I connected to the plane's WIFI and poked around online for a synagogue near our hotel, hoping for an egalitarian one where Travis and I would be able to sit next to one another. The egalitarian synagogue closest to our hotel in Boston was called, appropriately, the Boston Synagogue.

"It has to be a good one," Travis professed, "It's THE Boston Synagogue."

I rolled my eyes. "It will have to work," I said. I studied their website, and we arranged to attend Saturday morning services before heading to the center of Boston to ice-skate. I didn't bother to look up how long a Jewish service was expected to last nor what was actually going to happen. My friend Alana had once told me that it was similar to a church service, so I assumed we'd adapt on the fly.

On Friday afternoon, in the elevator of the Langham Hotel, I casually asked Travis what he was "wearing to synagogue." The words felt strange in my mouth. I felt like an imposter. (For the record, now I ask what he is planning to wear to "*shul*" or "services," but I don't think it was strictly word choice that made it feel so off that weekend).

"I don't know, I guess a dress shirt," he suggested, waiting for me to confirm whether this was appropriate.

"Let's go business casual," I decided. "Better to overdress than underdress."

On Saturday morning, we arrived at the synagogue doors at ten a.m. sharp. This was our first rookie mistake. If services start at ten, most of the congregation will drift in at a quarter to eleven. One of my Jewish acquaintances recently joked that if you show up at 11:50, you're still early for lunch. That explains why we didn't see anyone around when we approached the large brown building from behind. We walked up to the double doors and found that they were locked. There was a sign on the left side of the double doors proclaiming that all were welcome, and a sign on the right side of the double doors asking that visitors ring the bell so that an usher could identify them before allowing them in.

This trip came on the heels of a large synagogue shooting at Tree of Life Synagogue in Pittsburgh. Naturally, the community would feel the need to tighten security. I felt bad for not realizing that a surprise visitor might cause some anxiety. I considered scrapping the services idea and going straight to the ice-skating rink. Before we could flee, an older gentleman in a checkered suit shuffled to the door, grinning warmly.

"Welcome!" he exclaimed, thrusting open the doors, "Visitors! Come on in. We'll have a minyan soon and we'll start to pray."

"Great, sounds good," I replied awkwardly. I wondered if I should ask about what a minyan was, but I didn't.

"Where are you visiting from?" he asked as he led us down the hallway.

"Chicago," I said, debating whether or not to point out that we'd never actually gone to a synagogue in Chicago.

We shuffled along behind him until we reached the end of the entryway and emerged into the sanctuary. The "sanctuary" in this case consisted of a handful of chairs surrounding a podium, flanked by a large kitchen on one side and what looked like a small banquet hall on the other. The room was simple, and there were shelves overflowing with books absolutely everywhere. I had to side-step multiple racks of books in order to find a place to stand.

"Oh, Chicago, wonderful city," our host gushed. He didn't ask where we attended services in Chicago, so I didn't say anything. "Our fearless rabbi is out of town," he added, his voice apologetic. "She goes to Harvard and headed home for holiday break, so one of our congregants will lead the service."

I smiled politely and nodded, though this information made no sense. Churches have guest speakers from time to time, but the idea of a non-clergy member leading a religious service was as foreign to me as Hebrew. We made small talk with our host without mentioning that we were not Jewish. In my defense, it didn't come up. When the assembled members of the congregation made their way over to their chairs and picked up prayer books, we did the same.

"Do you need a prayer shawl?" he asked enthusiastically. I shook my head in response. I had an inkling that non-Jews were not supposed to touch the tattered prayer shawls hanging up on a hook near the ront door. Instead, our host handed us prayer books. I assumed that those were good for the taking. I opened the book and searched frantically for any indication of what we were supposed to be looking at. I quickly realized that we needed to read right to left instead of left to right, but I was used to this from my college Arabic classes.

After clearing his throat, the gentleman leading services began to chant in Hebrew. I tried to see what page of the prayer book that everyone else was looking at, but ultimately decided to focus on the chanting and to hum along wordlessly. The chanting continued, and continued, and continued. This was clearly not an "opening hymn," so to speak. Occasionally, I'd turn to a new page in my book to keep things fresh. Travis gave up on flipping through his book and started rocking back and forth on his heels, gently swaying to the rhythm of the chanting.

"I don't know what's happening," he whispered. But he looked content enough.

An hour went by and it became clear to me that services were not about to wrap up... they were still getting started. While Travis and I listened politely to the leader, the elderly congregants around us began to break off into casual side conversation. Our host and the woman sitting beside him starting gossiping about some congregant who had recently acquired a puppy. They were talking at full volume, apparently not concerned that the chanting was still very much in process. Someone else tapped our shoulder to ask about where we were visiting from. She didn't bother to whisper, but I did.

"We're from Chicago," I whispered, my palms sweating nervously at the prospect of talking during a religious service, "And we're converts," I added conspiratorially.

"Oh, that's amazing!" she exclaimed, completely undeterred. "We have plenty of converts here." She didn't point them out if they were in the room. In Judaism, it's considered improper to draw attention to a convert's status. Once you convert, it's like you had always been Jewish.

"Good to know," I whispered back, starting to feel less like an outsider already. As I was getting back to the prayer book that I couldn't read, I felt a THWACK against my right shoulder. I turned around. An old woman in a red suit was trying to get my attention and had smacked me with her purse. I turned around and raised my eyebrows in surprise.

"Are you going to stay for *kiddush*?" she asked innocently. "We'd love for you to stay for *kiddush*."

"Sure," I answered with a smile, clueless as to what *kiddush* was but hoping that it had something to do with snacks. I turned to the front once more, lowering my expectations about how much I'd be able to absorb. True to my prediction, I was soon interrupted by a shout.

"HEY! HE'S AHEAD OF US!" our host called out loudly, flipping frantically through his own prayer book. At least I wasn't the only one lost.

"My throat is dry," the service leader announced mid-prayer in a thick Israeli accent, "I'm going to go get some tea." At this, he walked off the stage and disappeared into the kitchen in the back of the room. My husband looked at me with wide eyes and let out a laugh.

"What is happening?" he whispered to me.

"I have no idea," I told him.

At random intervals, other people would set aside their prayer books and head to the kitchen for water or tea, as well. I stayed rooted to my spot near the back, watching the events unfold. It was, despite being beautiful, the most chaos I had ever seen in a place of worship. My husband had returned to his prayer book and was flipping through the pages of Hebrew to the English translations. He read silently. I couldn't gauge what he was thinking. When our fearless leader was back with a steaming cup of Lipton tea, it was time to start the Torah service. Our host offered us a chance to open the ark, which is where the Torah is stored while not being used. The only problem was, I obviously didn't know how to properly get the Torah out of the ark.

At this point I finally had my window of opportunity to announce that we were clueless converts who would not be participating in these services in any meaningful way.

"We're converting," I said quickly, "we can't go up there yet." I gestured vaguely at the front of the room where the prayer leader was waiting for the ark to be opened. The sacred space that surrounded the Torah scroll—that wasn't for us yet.

Our fellow congregants were not concerned.

"Ah!" our host said lightly, "You're studying then. Pay attention!" With a wink, he grabbed two different volunteers and the service was back underway.

If the opening psalms had been light and casual, the Torah service was orderly and prayerful. I watched the Torah readers rotate around the *bimah*, reading in melodic, unbroken Hebrew from the giant scroll. I was blown away by how unfamiliar everything was. It was nothing like Mass.

When the Torah service ended, there were more prayers. It was almost 12:30 p.m. when we wandered over to the bread and wine table to begin *kiddush*. I had really underestimated the time commitment here. *Kiddush*, though, was well worth staying for. After praying over the bread and wine, we sat down to a lunch of tuna salad, bagels, and chocolate cake. Everyone was excited to hear that we were embarking upon a journey of conversion.

"What's on your reading list?" our host asked, cutting himself a second piece of chocolate cake. I rattled off the list of books that I had yet to start, as well as a list of books that I'd already read. When I finished, he shook his head.

"That's a lot of books," someone interjected. "Do you think everyone here read all of that stuff? No! We were born Jewish and most of us are about as well-studied as this bagel. You shouldn't have to read all that."

"It's not a problem," I insisted, "I'm eager to learn."

"Oh, it's easy. It's all the golden rule!" our host exclaimed brightly. "Treat other people the way you want to be treated. The rest of it is all details." The rest of the table nodded in agreement.

I liked these people very much. We ended up skipping ice-skating to spend the afternoon chatting with our new friends. They asked us to come back once we had converted, and we promised to do so.

I was nervous that Travis would be turned off, but he was glowing after our visit to the synagogue. He found the chaos charming and the company refreshing. I felt a hopeful spark that he would choose to join me in conversion after all.

The rest of our vacation passed in a blur. On the last night of our trip, we made a reservation to eat at PABU, a trendy sushi spot on Franklin Street. In an abundance of caution, I ordered us everything except shellfish, which isn't part of a kosher diet. It was never too early to start practicing.

We headed back to Chicago feeling anxious to get our formal learning underway. I was still processing the Boston Synagogue experience. It differed so much from any Christian service I had ever been to. I wasn't sure I would ever catch up in Hebrew, and I wondered how I was going to survive long Saturday services instead of the typical hour-long Mass. I could think this conversion to death, but what was clear after our experience in Boston was that the best strategy was to summon our courage and dive in with both feet.

As we made last-minute preparations for the class, Travis finally asked the question that we had ignored up to this point: whether the Conservative movement was right for us.

"Are we stuck with them forever?" he asked, "What are they all about?"

I admitted that it was a good question. The American Jewish scene is dominated by several types of Judaism: Orthodoxy, Conservative Judaism, Reform Judaism, Reconstructionism. Ironically, the Boston Synagogue is non-affiliated, so we didn't even have a benchmark for where our interests might be.

The program near us happened to be Conservative, but it also felt like the right move for us. It felt to me like a middle-of-the-road option between the Reform and Orthodox movements although plenty of people would take issue with trying to place movements of Judaism on any sort of spectrum. For what it's worth, Anshe Emet's website made it clear that you could always shift your affiliation after completing the program. I understood, however, that becoming Orthodox is more complicated if your conversion was not overseen by Orthodox rabbis. I explained as much to Travis.

"Maybe we should do an Orthodox conversion," Travis suggested, "So that we don't get left out. I don't want to convert and not be fully Jewish. I don't want my kids' conversion to be questioned."

"You're converting now?" I asked, eyebrows raised.

"It's hypothetical," he sighed.

We did consider it, of course. I had nightmares about a Jewish summer camp denying my daughter a place or being told that my rabbi wouldn't perform a funeral for myself or Travis because our conversion wasn't "good enough."

I spent a lot of time trying to tease out the difference between varying levels of observance. The fact that women and men sit separately at Orthodox services and that women don't count toward a prayer quorum (a *minyan*) made us lean heavily back toward Conservative Judaism. Besides that, the main reason for me turning away from an Orthodox conversion was the dishonesty of it. I wouldn't be going through an Orthodox conversion for the right reasons. I knew that my observance would look more like that of the Conservative Jews at Anshe Emet, so doing our conversion with the movement we planned to affiliate with seemed like it was the right and most honest approach. I fully believe that there are few things more holy than our promises. I wanted to be able to give my word that I'd participate fully and enthusiastically in the norms of my community—the Conservative movement was the place where that promise would ring most true. I admire and respect Orthodox Judaism; in fact, we enthusiastically sent our daughter to a Chabad preschool. Other potential converts often ask how to pick a movement before their conversion. I tell them to go with the one that feels like home but to stay open to learning from other movements, too.

As a Jew, I enjoy drinking up knowledge from every movement of Judaism and appreciating the beauty found in each movement's teachings. Being a good neighbor means celebrating the diversity of belief and observance that exists in the Jewish world. Notably, I sometimes relate to the Orthodox teaching or perspective (or the Reform perspective) more than that of the Conservative movement on a given issue. I think that taking in a ton of information and being critical of all of it is a healthy approach.

There are certain people—let's call them seekers—who search and search for the "perfect" religion and never settle on one. I don't think these people are flighty or insincere, but I didn't want to be one of them. In deciding to become Jewish, I had to give myself permission to stop trying to find the one perfect religion or movement. Not having all of the answers is scary; not having all of the answers is freeing. Part of the reason that I was leaving Christianity in the first place was that there is too much pressure to accept Christian teachings as the ultimate universal Truth. I liked that I could grapple a little more with Jewish ideas, and the Jews around me are almost too gleeful to participate in the fiery debate.

To some people, this begs the question: why convert to a new religion at all if you're not going to accept every single belief that your new religion professes? To understand the answer this question, you have to understand the ways in which Judaism fundamentally differs from Christianity. For one, Jews don't even agree among themselves on most topics. In any case, you can reject certain tenets of the Jewish faith and still be in good standing with most movements of Judaism. For example, Jewish law isn't necessarily anti-death penalty (if it could be administered fairly), but I'm a staunch death penalty abolitionist. This doesn't mean I'm out of favor with Judaism. Although Jews don't mix chicken and dairy based on the laws of *kashrut*, I know Jews who shrug off the rule and do it anyway. Some Jews believe that God created the universe, and others subscribe to purely scientific theories. Ask two Jews, get three opinions.

If Christian doctrine felt to me like a tight, itchy sweater, Judaism felt like a soft, fuzzy robe. While a Christian might tell you that you're wrong when your ideas don't match up with Church doctrine, most Jews are willing to offer the divine a bit of constructive criticism where scripture is concerned. The word *Israel* itself means "to wrestle with God." I had been wrestling for quite some time. I was eager to get my hands dirty.

CHAPTER 10

"When we are no longer able to change a
situation, we are challenged to change ourselves."
—*Viktor Frankl*

As my nerves increased before my first class, I reached out to my friend Alana. I wanted her to be the first person to know about our conversion. Alana is a fiercely loyal social worker who has always been heavily involved in the Jewish community. She had been my roommate when I lived in graduate housing at the University of Michigan, and we became fast friends. By fast, I mean that within an hour of me dropping my bags on the floor of my room in our shared apartment, I felt like I'd known her forever. I knew that she would handle my news with grace even if she was caught by surprise. When I called her on the phone, I told her that even if she thought it was a terrible idea, the conversion course was starting in a matter of days and I was going to be there for it. As it happens, she didn't think it was a bad idea at all.

"The only thing is," she pointed out brightly, "you know, we're happy to have you, but have you thought about the fact that your children are going to be a religious minority and thus face rampant and growing antisemitism? Not trying to dissuade you, just wondering if you thought this out, you know?" You can always count on Alana to present the possibility of antisemitism in as upbeat a tone as possible.

"It has crossed my mind," I admitted, "But if the one thing that stops me from converting is antisemitism, I'll always feel like antisemitism won. And it shouldn't."

"In that case," said Alana, "Yay! Welcome to the tribe! I can't wait to hear everything about what you're learning."

"I'll keep you posted," I promised. With one official Jewish person's blessing to convert, I was ready to start studying. I had already finished Kushner's *To Life*, so I switched to Heschel's *Sabbath* and started watching Shalom Sesame videos—meant obviously for children—to memorize the Jewish aleph-bet.

In order to make us feel welcome before the new semester, Liz Berke invited Travis and me to a Shabbat dinner at her home. This is something that Liz does frequently. She invites total strangers who are curious about Judaism to sit at her family's table and enjoy a meal. As fate would have it, I had a work event that I couldn't wiggle out of. I asked Travis if he would go to dinner on his own as our official representative. Despite having had a good time at the Boston Synagogue, this struck him as patently absurd.

"This was YOUR idea!" he said. "And you're going to send ME to dinner alone at the cantor's house? I don't know how to do a Shabbat dinner!"

"I think you, you know, eat dinner," I pointed out helpfully. "It will give you a chance to meet the cantor and ask questions without me. You're much friendlier than I am, anyway," I told him in an effort to butter him up. It was true. Travis is far more extroverted than I am and far more susceptible to the promise of a free home-cooked meal.

"Okay, I'll go," he agreed.

The dinner must have gone well because he came home that night seeming very optimistic about the conversion process. I even caught him looking at challah recipes online later that week.

By the time the evening of our first class rolled around, we had built up a lot of anticipation. The classroom was almost entirely full by the time that we arrived. For organizational purposes, Anshe Emet's class coincided with the standard academic calendar though students are welcome to join, or drop, at any point. Most of the students were already familiar with one another because they had started in September.

I looked around and assessed my classmates. A few of us were new, but most students had been studying for a while and came armed with Hebrew name tags and wearing *kippot* [often called a "yarmulke"]. Some students had come with a spouse or partner while a smaller handful attended on their own. I scooped up a name tag and wrote my name in English.

For all of the nerves and anticipation, conversion classes were very low-key. They mostly involved lectures and conversations; no pop-quizzes, no being put on the spot about our knowledge. Our first class was a guest lecture presenting a survey of Jewish art. The lecturer had prepared a PowerPoint. I whipped out my notepad and jotted down a couple of notes like I was in a college class. I had never given much thought to Jewish art, but it was a digestible-enough topic to start with. Art was familiar and approachable. The guest lecturer showed us slides of Jewish art and contrasted the paintings with Christian art from the same time periods. Christian art is so prevalent in our culture—in churches, of course, but also in museums, textbooks, home goods stores, films. I couldn't believe how little Jewish art I'd laid my eyes on. Travis nodded along with the lecture, and I kept taking notes. The lecturer stopped early to let us ask questions or share our thoughts, but it was also perfectly fine for us to not talk if we didn't wish to. All in all, our first class was a hit.

On Saturday, we returned to the synagogue for our next scheduled class. When I entered the classroom, I grabbed the attendance sheet and looked around for a pen.

"You sign in by putting a sticker by your name," Liz instructed with a patient smile. "We don't write on Shabbat because writing is an act of creation."

"Oh," I said slowly, considering this news. I knew I wasn't supposed to use my phone in the synagogue, but all of the "rules" about what to do and not do on the Sabbath were unfamiliar. I made a mental note to look into it later. Were we not supposed to have taken the CTA to the synagogue? What about the coffee I paid for at the Coffee

Tree on my way to class? I was holding the evidence of my Sabbath crime in my hands. I quietly tucked the coffee cup under my chair and waited for class to begin.

The day's topic was the process of becoming Bar or Bat Mitzvah. I was amazed to find out that the ceremony and the big afterparty were not required. Girls *become* Bat Mitzvah, or a daughter of the commandments, when they wake up on their 12th birthday, party or no party. Boys *become* Bar Mitzvah the same way on their 13th birthday.

No matter how much I had read beforehand, I really knew nothing. As Liz patiently explained the process of being called up to the Torah, I had a moment of panic where I told myself that it was too much information to catch up on. I didn't know *aleph* from *bet*. I had never been to a bar or bat mitzvah celebration. I purchased coffee on the Sabbath! Setting my jaw in determination, I returned my focus to the prayer handout and tried my best to follow along. I snuck a sip of coffee, too. This was going to be a long journey. I needed to be caffeinated.

This first week paints an accurate picture of what the conversion program was like on a week-to-week basis. I often get more questions about how conversion works than about why I converted. I understand that because I had the same questions myself before I began. How you convert largely depends on which movement of Judaism oversees your conversion, but for us, it looked like taking a lot of these classes at the synagogue and beginning to "live Jewishly" at home. Some days I would feel that I was starting to understand things when I answered a question right during class, and other days I would get panicky about not remembering every section of the *Amidah*, a long prayer composed of nineteen blessings. Liz assured me that this was normal. Learning is a lifelong commitment, and confidence is not always linear.

Our courses at Anshe Emet involved Hebrew and Jewish culture on Monday evenings, and Jewish religion lessons on Saturday mornings, e.g., in our first week, art on Monday and the concept of becoming Bat Mitzvah on Saturday. Our course packed in a lot more Jewishness outside of those two weekly classes: one-on-one meetings with rabbinical staff, Hebrew lessons, reading assignments, Jewish home practice steps, Shabbat dinners, volunteer work, and assorted field trips. Classes are important, but being Jewish is something that you *do* as much as it's something that you *know*. The home practice is significant, more so than in Christianity. It sounds like quite a long list of requirements, and it is, but I don't recall feeling particularly overwhelmed. The only thing I could do was take my conversion one day at a time, and that's what I did.

Given our tight schedules, Travis and I chose to teach ourselves Hebrew at home. I ordered an *Aleph Isn't Tough* workbook online and promised myself that I would do one chapter per week. The schedule was ambitious. On Mondays, I would work at my law firm until 6:30 p.m., at which time I'd run to the CTA Brown Line and arrive fashionably late for our 7pm class. On Saturdays, we would wake up less than an hour before class and shove stale challah into our mouths on our way outside to catch the bus. I felt like I was always literally on the run. I taught myself Hebrew whenever I had a window, usually on Sunday mornings. I would send Alana videos of me reading short sentences in slow, butchered Hebrew. I understood the sounds that the letters made, but I often emphasized the wrong syllables.

"The words were right that time, but the cadence was off," she pointed out gently when I sent her a recording of the blessing over Shabbat candles. Most Jewish prayers are set to a specific cadence that becomes as natural as breathing once you pick it up. She sent back a voice recording of her much better rendition, and I used that to continue practicing.

I read my way through the book list on Shabbat—when we were supposed to avoid electronics, work, writing, and cooking. In the darkness of our apartment, Travis and I would munch on Cheez-Its and read. I read books about Jewish funerals, Jewish holidays, the laws of keeping kosher, the Holocaust. On weekday mornings I would read while running on an elliptical at the East Bank Club, squinting at the tiny print while my legs churned wildly below. I flew through the program's reading list and ordered five, then ten, then fifteen additional books. I finished Milton Steinberg's *As a Driven Leaf* in three days flat.

"This is a very Jewish way to behave," Liz joked. "Your bookshelf is going to topple over."

Anshe Emet was a wonderful place to study. It had a homey feeling. The synagogue consisted of a gymnasium, multiple classrooms, offices for staff, and a beautiful sanctuary with arched ceilings and a stunning stained-glass mural on the back wall that reminded me vaguely of a church.

The largest notable difference was the security wall surrounding the synagogue and the security check-in desks at every entrance. That took some adjustment. When I was growing up, my Catholic church never had anything in the way of security. The front door was propped open even in the heart of winter. I would sometimes make a game plan in my head for what I would do if someone broke into Anshe Emet's sanctuary with a gun, and then I'd quickly chastise myself for "being dramatic." I didn't know what to make of my own security in Jewish spaces. Over time, I began to feel as safe at Anshe Emet as I felt at St. Thomas growing up.

Conversion classes became something that I looked forward to, no matter how busy I was at work. Liz Berke led the program with much passion but no expectation that any individual student would convert in the end. Liz was endlessly patient and unassuming. She asked us as many questions as we asked her. This is a very Jewish thing to do: to ask questions and invite students to weigh in on topics of which they know little. I grew to appreciate this even when I felt out of my depths. Liz gave us journaling prompts but never asked to read our reflections. We were given a surprising amount of privacy about our own conversions. I expected to be grilled at every step of the process about my beliefs. Surely, someone would be checking in to ensure that I believed the "right" things? But Liz simply taught. Conversations about changing beliefs and worldviews were scheduled one on one with rabbis where we could privately discuss the finer points of our Jewish belief system without an audience.

As more Monday classes flew by, we covered Jewish history, Sephardic culture, the concept of *tikkun olam* [repairing the world], Jewish views on sex and intimacy. We reviewed the basics of major Jewish holidays and attended guest lectures about things like the Jewish presence in Asia and Africa. We only had half a class period that covered the State of Israel, and Liz let the students do all of the talking. Although non-Jews are constantly fixated on my views of Israel and Palestine, it simply wasn't a cornerstone of the conversion coursework. There was nothing more frustrating than announcing my conversion to someone and being instantly asked to opine on Israel and nothing else.

Judaism is so much more than a religion, and Monday night classes made that clear. Judaism is a peoplehood, a covenant, a system of ethics, a religion, and a guide to living a meaningful life. Understanding the history and composition of the Jewish community was important to learn hand-in-hand with the contents of the Torah. So, much of our Monday night classes had more to do with understanding Jews than understanding the tenets of the Jewish faith (though the two are connected). We learned which gifts are customary for Purim, the geography of world Jewry, the layout of a standard synagogue, and what most Jews make for dinner for their Passover seders. Monday night classes ensured that I would understand topics of conversations among my "culturally" Jewish friends as well as I would understand the stories in the Torah.

We were supposed to have a class on antisemitism, and we sort of did. A guest speaker asked us to raise our hands if we worried about antisemitism. A number of hands went up.

"It doesn't worry me," he said, "I can't change it." We all waited for him to elaborate, but somehow the topic shape-shifted until he was gushing about the beauty of Jerusalem and wishing us "*laila tov*" [good night] because class was over for the night.

Saturdays were more focused on religious topics and events. We learned to sing and pray like Jews by focusing on the *Shema* and *Amidah*, two of the hallmark prayers in the Jewish service. The *Shema* is a declaration of the oneness of God followed by particular versus about how Jews are to live their faith. The *Amidah* is a prayer of both petition (asking something from God) and thankfulness (thanking God). Many Jewish prayers are designed to be communal, so knowing the cadence and meaning of certain Jewish prayers is essential to feeling at home during a Jewish service. We also learned how to say a blessing before a Torah reading and specific prayers and songs that might be recited at major events like a wedding or *bris*. Because doing can be better than merely discussing, we performed very convincing fake weddings, divorces, baby-naming ceremonies, and even a *bris* of an unsuspecting stuffed pig. We engaged in discussions about weekly Torah readings, and we had an entire class devoted to the many names for God in Judaism and what those names can teach us about how Jews view the divine.

Classes were often done lecture-style, but we had ample time to talk in pairs with other converts. I was happily surprised to learn that less than half of my peers were converting for marriage. Many, like me, felt called to a Jewish life despite not having been raised in a Jewish environment. Some of them were formerly Christian, some were not. Our cohort included members of the LGBT community, a mother and child from Latin America, and several spouses of potential converts who enjoyed re-learning things about the Jewish tradition. For some people, the decision to convert to Judaism had been made before they attended their first class. That's how it felt for me. The classes were a confirmation of what I knew was the right path for me.

Our first in-class Jewish holiday was a somewhat odd one: Tu B'Shevat. This holiday falls in the early winter and celebrates the new year for trees. We jokingly referred to it as Jewish Earth Day. To celebrate the holiday, we had a Tu B'Shevat seder where we ate nuts, dried fruit, and four glasses of grape juice in place of wine. I was pleasantly surprised by Judaism's focus on natural or agricultural events. I was used to Christian holidays being tied to strictly divine events like the birth and death of Jesus. Judaism's connection to the natural world and cycles of growth and harvest was very grounding for me. I went home after the seder and reminded all of my actually raised-Jewish friends that if they were failing to celebrate the new year for trees, they were missing out.

"I dig this holiday," Travis chirped as he read more about it in our holiday text book. "Judaism seems to really prioritize care of the environment and an understanding of the natural world."

Even as your knowledge base grows as an early convert, jumping into the Jewish world can be intimidating. The Jews are a somewhat insular group with a long, turbulent history. I was in awe of everyone's conviction and willingness to put themselves out there. I tried to emulate their confidence and enthusiasm. I don't know what each and every one of my classmates believed about God or Jewish law. It would be inappropriate for me to ask since I wasn't one of the rabbis who would ultimately sit on their *beit din*.

I always felt like there was room to discuss the contours of my beliefs without the rabbinical staff being judgmental. Our classroom discussions were lively without being pushy. I cherished the perspective of my classmates and was relieved that we need not agree on everything to form a community with one another.

On one Saturday, Rabbi David Russo invited us to join his preservice Torah study with older members of the congregation. Parashah classes involve reading a small portion of the Torah and arguing about its meaning as a group. It's similar to what Christians call a Bible study. Although Christians adopted what they refer to as the "Old Testament" and read from it regularly, I was constantly finding that I hadn't read the same stories that you hear in Jewish spaces, or at least not in the same way.

This week's reading was *Parashat Terumah*, where God gives the wandering Israelites instructions on how to build a Tabernacle in the wilderness. This story took us to the desert where the Israelites were taking in instructions on precisely how to construct their mobile Tabernacle. The story reads like an intricate blueprint. God tells the Israelites to gather acacia wood, colorful yarn, linen, copper, gold, oil. Oh, also some dolphin skins. My brow wrinkled in confusion: *Dolphin skins? In the desert?* This conundrum had not come up in Sunday School. Jews are working from a very different translation of the text, and on top of that tend to hone in on much different details. I had to stretch myself to keep up.

Rabbi Russo let out a chuckle at the mysterious translation and asked the class to start dissecting what the translation could mean. The conversion students went silent and looked to the other congregants to answer. I had no idea, so I patiently waited for a smarter Jew to impart their knowledge. A variety of ideas were advanced. They were dolphin skins that had been salvaged from the Red Sea during the Israelites' exodus from Egypt. It was the skin of a different animal that the text had mistranslated. The animal the text spoke of was extinct. It was not skin at all, but some blue linen or yarn.

"I don't think anyone needed a dolphin in the desert," a blonde woman interjected confidently, leaning back in her chair. "They're probably talking about something dyed blue. I don't think the Torah is *true*. I think it's a nice story and the point of the story is that the tabernacle is supposed to be beautiful. That's all."

"I hope it was a mythical creature that's extinct now," another woman with gray hair and a bright blue cardigan admitted with a sly smile. "Like a unicorn. I like that reading better."

We all looked at the rabbi to gauge his reaction. To our surprise, he nodded enthusiastically. Everyone else nodded, too.

The class moved on without the rabbi offering any insight as to what he thought the passage meant. We didn't all have to agree on one interpretation for the class to be considered a success. I was so relieved that I could have wept.

CHAPTER 11

"The great aim of education is not knowledge but action." —*Herbert Spencer*

When we weren't in the classroom poring over books and prayers, we were taking field trips to explore Jewishness around Chicago.

One of our first trips was to a local Reform temple, Temple Sholom. I hadn't seen many American synagogues, so when we arrived for Friday night services, I made a point of taking in all of the differences between Anshe Emet and Temple Sholom. Anshe Emet was dark and cozy, while Temple Sholom was bright and massive. Temple Sholom had cavernous ceilings and long, winding hallways. We met in their large social hall for wine and snacks before services began. I had come to really appreciate all of the free drinks that Jewish spaces offer. Travis and I sipped on white wine and munched on raw vegetables as the rest of our classmates arrived.

When the sanctuary was open for services, we marched in as a group, frantically flipping through the Reform prayer books (called *siddurim*) to see if they were familiar to us. Reform prayer services tend to make more use of English or the relevant local language in addition to Hebrew. There were also nonreligious texts in these particular books, such as poems written in a secular context but included for their beauty and thoughtfulness. I flipped through it and was relieved that I was less lost than usual.

The rabbi who led the service did so with upbeat guitar music and summer camp-style arm waving, and she kindly dropped English instructions into the major Hebrew prayers of the service. Conservative synagogues mostly do not use instruments, so it was a nice change of pace. Toward the end of the service, a young couple was called up for an *aufruf*, an Ashkenazic practice where engaged couples are prayed over and showered in handfuls of candy before their wedding. The candy is supposed to symbolize a "sweet life" for the couple. Family members beamed, and children continued to run about. There was an energy and joy to the service that made it a lovely way to bring in the Sabbath.

We later ventured to an Orthodox service on our own in order to compare it with the other services we had grown familiar with. Travis was distraught about being separated from me by the *mechitzah*, so he sat immediately next to the sheer curtain so that we could peer at each other through it.

"We're going to get in trouble," I groaned. "Don't talk to me! Don't look at me!"

"I don't know what page we're on," he said through the curtain, "It's all in Hebrew."

As if he had overheard, the rabbi began to call out page numbers. The other men turned and stared blankly at Travis, assessing whether he was the source of the sudden page number calling. He blushed and buried his head in a prayer book.

Life on the women's side of the aisle was more laid back. Other women sat around me in skirts and fancy hats, flipping peacefully through their prayer books. A kind older woman kept turning around to show me which page we were on. Most of it went over my head, but it was a good point of reference.

Our next trip was to the Wilmette community *mikveh*. The *mikveh* is used for ritual immersion in Jewish life, but more significantly, it was the place where we would complete our conversions. The *mikveh* was a small bathing chamber attached to the synagogue, complete with its own shower room and towel racks. It was warm and inviting. The *mikveh* attendant talked us through the history of the *mikveh*.

"We built this *mikveh* ourselves to the exact specifications required by Jewish law," she explained, her eyes twinkling with delight, "it is three cubits deep, one cubit wide, and one cubit long, with 150 gallons of naturally occurring water. In this case, frozen blocks of spring water."

We all nodded our heads with great interest. Everything in Judaism is so wonderfully precise.

"Do we wear bathing suits when we immerse?" one of my classmates asked.

"Quite the opposite," she explained, smiling patiently. "The waters of the *mikveh* must touch every part of you. You have to be completely naked. You're by yourself, and the *mikveh* attendant will hold up a towel for privacy. You will shower before getting into the *mikveh*. You must be free of all cosmetics, lotion, nail polish, dirt beneath the nails, contact lenses, and jewelry." I looked down at my purple nail polish. Totally bare. Got it. I snatched up one of her handouts so that I wouldn't forget the rules. I was more excited than ever to take my first trip to those waters as part of my conversion.

"I want to convert outside, in a lake or something," one of my classmates gushed. She was a thin, wistful young woman, very into yoga and organic eating, so converting in the ocean or a lake seemed on-brand for her.

"That creates some modesty issues," the *mikveh* attendant admitted, "but it can be arranged if that's what you want."

My classmate smiled broadly and settled back into her seat.

"I want to do it inside," I whispered to Travis, "Less distractions." I had seen videos of people being baptized in large bodies of water. I suppose it seemed romantic, even Biblical, but it also seemed like a lot of chaos. I didn't need more chaos.

"Agreed," Travis whispered back.

"You've never said you were coming to the *mikveh*," I teased, jabbing him in the ribs.

"Of course I am," he replied, brow furrowed in confusion. "How else would I convert?"

"Okay, Mr. I'm-just-here-for-the-classes," I laughed.

Travis was taking to Judaism like a fish to water. He was ahead of me in Hebrew and was outpacing me in the reading department. All he could talk about was how excited he was for the Sabbath every week. I was impressed by his enthusiasm.

"He's going to end up being a rabbi," Liz teased later that morning as we headed back to our cars.

"Who would have thought," I said to no one in particular.

After the *mikveh* trip, our next event involved serving with the Night Ministry in Lakeview. The Night Ministry is a Chicago organization that provides housing, health care, and other social services to adults and youth who struggle with homelessness and poverty. The Night Ministry provides over 75,000 meals a year to those in need. The Night Ministry is able to provide consistent, reliable service with the help of local volunteers. The program is longstanding and well-organized.

I considered the ways in which it was similar to PBJ Outreach back in Detroit. Older and wiser, I researched the sustainability of the Night Ministry and the work they do to bring an end to poverty and homelessness. I was happy to be learning more about how to best serve vulnerable communities instead of showing up without a clue.

In Cantor Berke's dining room, we made an assembly line of volunteers, placing turkey and cheese onto slices of bread with gloved hands and wrapping the sandwiches tightly in a layer of foil. Jews don't mix milk and meat, and the turkey we were making the sandwiches with wasn't kosher. They didn't have to be. We were serving people who would be happier to eat a sandwich with cheese than without, and so we met that need regardless of whether it comported with Jewish law. (But notably, we covered the Cantor's counter in saran wrap as to not compromise the laws of kashrut in her space). After preparing the sandwiches, we bundled up and headed outside to help the Night Ministry staff ladle the hot soup into individual cups and set up long tables with oranges and fresh-baked cookies. With us was a preteen girl who had helped organize our volunteer efforts as part of her Bat Mitzvah project. As I helped her transfer the soup from our oversized pot into small to-go containers, she asked me something that no one had asked since my meeting with Cantor Berke.

"Why do you want to be Jewish?" she asked curiously. She kept filling the to-go containers while she waited for my answer.

"Oh, wow," I said. "Well, that's quite a question."

"You don't have to answer," she offered kindly. "I've been preparing for my Bat Mitzvah, and a rabbi asked me last week if I believed in God. I said no. I said no because there's no proof unless you count that burning bush, which I don't, by the way." She glanced sideways at me to gauge my reaction.

"I believe in a different God than I used to," I said carefully. "The Jewish concept of God is refreshingly complicated. But more than that, I believe in the Jewish community. I think that Jews have a very unique way of looking at our days on earth and finding ways to make them holy. Have you read Heschel? He writes about the practice of sanctifying time. Sanctifying the act of eating by remembering to say a blessing, sanctifying it by acknowledging where your meat and milk came from. He talks about sanctifying time by lighting candles at sundown on Friday, and sanctifying the passage of time by celebrating Rosh Hashanah and Yom Kippur. I want to be Jewish because I want my time on earth to be spent carefully and with attention to the world around me. I think that's important, even if there is no God. In fact, I think it's even more important if there's no God and no world after this one."

My new friend considered this explanation. It might have been my best answer yet, come to think of it.

"That makes sense," she said thoughtfully. "I like that Judaism is about giving back to the community and healing the wrongs of the world. And I like summer camp. Plus, no one forces you to believe certain things. It's pretty chill."

"Trying to make teenagers believe anything is a fool's errand," I replied with a wink. It is admirable to give your child the gift of faith, and even more admirable to give them the autonomy to question it. Judaism was littered with pearls of wisdom like this, and I held on to every last one.

As we served the soup and sandwiches, we spent time talking with the Chicagoans who had come to eat. Some of them were recent immigrants trying to get on their feet; one woman was pregnant and couldn't afford enough healthy groceries to keep up with her growing appetite. Slowing down and treating the people you serve as human beings and not notches on your path to heaven is important. Night Ministry was a social experience. After being fed, everyone hovered around to socialize.

"We prefer peanut butter sandwiches," a kind gentleman explained to me as he took another cup of soup. "Peanut butter doesn't spoil, and turkey does. And oranges are great because the skin protects them, instead of apples that get beat up."

"Thank you for saying something," I told him. "I'm going to relay this to the synagogue and the Night Ministry staff. It's important."

"We like the candy and cookies though," he said, "Don't forget that—the sugar is good."

"The sugar is good," I agreed with a smile. "Have a great night."

"I like turkey," another woman chimed in, taking another sandwich.

"Maybe they can bring a combination next time," Travis told her. "The feedback is great. Thank you."

We had both come to understand that community service was meant to benefit the served, not the people serving. We wanted to make that part of our practice moving forward.

After our community service night, I got to return to Liz's house for a Shabbat dinner. Travis spent weeks perfecting his challah recipe and was proud to show up to the potluck with twin loaves of fresh-baked bread, carefully braided and adorned with sesame seeds. Fifteen to twenty of us sat around a large table, enjoying food and wine and good company by candlelight.

The dinner had the atmosphere of a holiday celebration. Shabbat is a holiday of sorts, I suppose. A holiday that comes around like clockwork every week to remind us to slow down and enjoy one another. How lucky was I to have a lifetime of little holidays awaiting me?

"I love Liz," Travis gushed when we left, "and I love Shabbat."

"Someone has really gotten enthusiastic about this conversion," I told him again.

"Yeah," he confirmed, "I can't believe how much I love what I'm learning. I can't believe I was so nervous about the possibility of conversion. I'm excited to be Jewish."

"Me, too," I professed.

After that Shabbat dinner, our last planned field trip was to the Illinois Holocaust Museum. The Holocaust, referred to as the *Shoah* by the community, is something that I was familiar with through ordinary American schooling. But knowing about the Holocaust and understanding the trauma that it caused to the Jewish world, and continues to cause through inherited intergenerational trauma, is a topic that must be approached with great care. Travis and I never lost relatives in the *Shoah* or to other vicious antisemitic violence throughout history. This does not mean that we cannot remember the victims of the *Shoah*; any person with a conscience should be heartbroken by the magnitude of cruelty and loss. But we had to approach the history of violence against Jews with an eye toward understanding how those events impacted the Jews who were direct descendants of survivors.

Of course, I had some additional experience with Holocaust history by virtue of having participated in FASPE. Travis was not with me when I toured Auschwitz the previous year with the program. I called Travis from my Polish hotel and stumbled over my words.

"There's a list," I told him. "A list of the names of all known victims of the Holocaust. The names are written on huge scrolls in this exhibit at Auschwitz. The scrolls were taller than me, and there were hundreds and hundreds of them. A room full of thin scrolls, filled with names. It was like walking through a forest of scrolls. I feel sick."

"It's terrible," he said softly. "I saw an exhibit at the Holocaust Museum in Washington D.C. It was shoes. Children's shoes. So many shoes. I felt sick, too."

"We spent the whole day here," I told him. "I read as many names as I could. I read plaques and poems. I stood in these terrible places and tried my hardest to focus my attention on all of the losses. But it's not enough. I could spend a week here and still not feel like I fully paid my respects."

"Yeah," Travis said sadly. I could tell that he was unsure about what to say. I had felt the same way all day.

"There's an ice cream shop in town here," I told him, flopping onto my bed and staring blankly at the ceiling. "It's like ... the town went on. People go out for pizza. And right down the road is this awful, disgusting place where thousands of innocent people were sent to their deaths."

"I ... I don't know," he said. "It's a lot to handle."

"We have a group meeting soon," I told him, "I'll call tomorrow."

I hung up and hauled myself out of bed. I needed a bit of fresh air before our meeting. When I stepped outside into the late afternoon light, I took a breath and looked up to the sky. *How can you shine here?* I wondered, squinting up at the sun above me. I was momentarily thankful that our meeting was going to be in a dark, damp basement conference room. The atmosphere complemented my mood nicely.

Our meeting was short. It involved more silence than talking. Our usually gregarious group was somber; our eminently thoughtful professors were lost in their own thoughts, too.

"The children's sweaters always get me," one of our professors said sadly. We all nodded, eyes trained on the stone floor below us. There was a lump in my throat. For once, I had nothing to contribute to the conversation.

"No one has to speak," another professor assured us. "We can sit here until dinnertime." And so that's what we did: we honored the victims of the *Shoah* with our silence, sitting in community with one another as we worked through the tangle of emotions within us.

I didn't eat well that night. I poked at my risotto and choked down a few sips of dry red wine. The other fellows made conversation over dinner; I was on edge and eager to call it a day.

When I curled up under my starchy hotel sheets after sunset, I found that I couldn't sleep. Visiting Auschwitz changes a lot of people, but for potential converts, it raises un-answerable questions about how to process and honor these dark periods in Jewish history. I scrapped the sleep idea and journaled instead, writing away until my hand cramped and my eyes drooped with sleep. I carefully tucked my journal under my pull-out bed and drifted off.

We left Oswiecim [Auschwitz] the next morning. My friend Sarah sat next to me on the bus and tried to make me smile with her sharp, witty comments. It started to work. The farther that we traveled from the camps, the more I could feel my shoulders relax and my lungs fill with air. The sunshine seemed brighter and more genuine as we got closer to the Krakow city center.

Don't forget what it felt like to be there, I scrawled in my journal before falling asleep again on Sarah's shoulder. She was infinitely more comfortable than the window to my right, but it was also nice to be touching someone.

* * *

Auschwitz is an immersive experience. It's difficult to be there because the horrors of the *Shoah* feel so present and immediate. The Illinois Holocaust Museum was, in comparison, a significantly less tumultuous experience. As my conversion cohort moved from exhibit to exhibit,

I watched my classmates take in facts about *Kristallnacht* and deportation.

I know, I kept thinking to myself, *because I was there.* I stood on the streets in Berlin where pogroms had been carried out. My feet touched the train platform where families had been torn apart. I saw the barbed wire fence that had roped in some of the survivors profiled on the museum's walls. I wondered if my fellow converts felt the weight of the Holocaust the way that I did after my trip, which was still quite far removed from the way that Jewish families touched directly by the atrocities must feel. My head started to swim with emotion again.

"We're going to go to the theater now," Liz announced, pulling me from my thoughts. "There is a presentation being made by a hologram of a survivor."

"Be right there," I called back, pulling myself away from an exhibit featuring a tiny replica of Auschwitz-Birkenau.

A hologram. That's all that the generations after mine will be left with as the survivors of the *Shoah* pass on. More and more, it is up to all of us to remember. Of course, we must let the families most affected by antisemitic violence drive the narrative. Sometimes, the best way to remember is to listen. And so we listened to the hologram, and then we went home.

The Holocaust was, to be sure, a melancholy topic even if it was an important one. But it wasn't all a discussion of persecution and discrimination. There was a lot of joy in becoming a Jew, too. There were the Shabbat potlucks, learning to fry up latkes, the gorgeous music at Saturday services. There was the joy of getting a clean slate on Yom Kippur and the silliness of planning a Purim costume.

Purim was the second holiday that we celebrated during our conversion course. Purim commemorates the Jews being saved from persecution in the ancient Persian Empire by the cunning and brave Queen Esther. Jews jokingly say things like, "they tried to kill us, we lived, let's drink" when talking about the theme of Purim. Purim celebrations are silly and raucous, with costumes being worn to represent that things are not as they seem (since Queen Esther strategically hid her Jewishness in order to save the Jewish people). Many non-Jews are familiar with *hamantaschen*, the cookie meant to represent that hat of the villain of the Purim story, Haman. Our job for the holiday was to volunteer at a children's Purim carnival, helping kids into and out of bouncy houses, watching them run around gleefully in their costumes and sneak *hamantaschen* behind their parents' backs. You would be surprised at how hard it is to find Halloween costumes in the middle of February, so I did not dress up. Their joy and pride in being Jewish was palpable. I would have to take the joy and the sorrow in equal measure.

As it turns out, the best way to start feeling like part of the Jewish community is simply to show up. The more I went to services and purchased my own Judaica sets, the more I started naturally feeling like I belong. It didn't have to be forced. Judaism absorbed me, and I learned by immersion how to blend in. There was, of course, the matter of telling everyone else that I was becoming Jewish. By the time Passover rolled around, I had only told Alana and my mother that we were converting. Claiming to be Jewish before going to the *mikveh* didn't feel right, but it's remarkably difficult to start following Jewish law if you have to do so in total secret. Per the program recommendations, we started small and built up. We purchased Shabbat candlesticks to use at home and lit the candles every Friday night. I made sure not to buy any non-kosher grocery products such as shrimp or non-kosher deli meat. Being Jewish out in the world was only slightly more nerve-wracking.

The first time Travis wore a *kippah* out in public, we ran into a former law school classmate of mine.

"Do you think she saw my *kippah*?" he asked nervously.

"Honestly," I told him, "I don't think she would remember you well enough to recall that you didn't used to wear one. I don't think people pay that much attention."

"By the way, we're not supposed to eat at restaurants on the Sabbath," he whispered. "Spending money on Shabbat is against the rules."

"Well," I said, licking some jam guiltily off of my toast, "I forgot. The man at the table next to us is wearing a *kippah* and dining out on the Sabbath, so I don't reckon we're going to be struck by lightning or anything." As if he had heard me, the man glanced at our table and noticed Travis's *kippah*.

"Shabbat Shalom," the man chirped, looking up with a smile from his matzoh ball soup. Travis beamed. Maybe this wasn't so hard after all.

After that, I felt like we were always on a scavenger hunt to see other people wearing *kippot* in public. A nice family taking a walk in New York City, a law school classmate in the library, the man who sat behind us at *Fiddler on the Roof* in downtown Chicago. Being Jewish—or almost Jewish—felt like belonging to a tight-knit club. Even though I never took to wearing a *kippah* myself, I did buy myself a colorful *hamsa* necklace, regarded by many Jews as protection against the evil eye. The symbol isn't exclusive to Judaism, but wearing it allowed me to give a quick nod to my new culture in a way that felt authentic for me.

In Judaism, the road to feeling like you belong is a long one. It's best to travel it one step at a time. That seemed to do the trick for us.

CHAPTER 12

"You cannot serve from an empty vessel." –
Eleanor Brownn

Learning the "rules" surrounding Shabbat and other Jewish customs came fairly easily. It was making decisions about how to build those Jewish customs into my life from scratch that proved to be difficult. Converts can't simply do what their parents did when it comes to religious observance. With no Jewish past to build from, converts are left to observe the thousands of combinations of Jewish practices adopted by fellow Jews, using a combination of rabbinical guidance and gut instincts to forge ahead.

Observing Shabbat came easily to me. The chance to log off and observe twenty-four hours of family time and personal reflection was irresistible. I was taken by the magic of Shabbat at my friend's family table back in Needham, Massachusetts during college, and the magic of Shabbat only grew as I learned to observe it in our own way. Of course, there were small decisions to navigate. Would we avoid all prohibited activities, including cooking, driving, spending money, "tearing" objects like paper, turning on lights, carrying objects outside of the home, and brushing our teeth or showering? Would we be available to work if the need was "significant"? I admit to being a teeth-brushing fanatic, but I eventually decided that work could live without me, even in a pinch.

On the whole, I enjoyed Shabbat. I would still Facetime my parents who lived in another state if there wasn't a better time to schedule the call for, but we found a way to observe that was both holy and felt like home to us.

Going to the *mikveh*, which many observant Jewish women describe as a pain in the *tuchus*, would become something that I looked forward to post-conversion. The *mikveh*, to me, was a miniature escape from parenting and a spa for the soul. Holidays were a joy to participate in, including making the oft-dreaded Yom Kippur apology calls wherein you phone up anyone that you wronged in the past 365 days and offer an apology. Attending long Saturday services was no big deal. The thing that I went back and forth on the most was keeping kosher.

I wasn't terribly attached to shellfish or bacon cheeseburgers; in fact, Travis and I mostly kept to a vegetarian diet anyway. The problem was that I had long since adopted a personal policy against food restrictions, however noble their purpose. I survived an eating disorder once, and I had learned that—for me—even light dietary restrictions can become a slippery slope to obsession. I wouldn't join my friends in doing The Whole30, nor keto, nor paleo, nor any of the other diets that came and went. But Liz asked that I at least try to keep kosher for a short time frame before completing my conversion, so I agreed to do so on a trial basis.

Contrary to conventional wisdom, my eating disorder never seemed to be about control alone, though that played its part, I'm sure. I imagine that the seed was planted when 11-year-old Shannon was quizzed by her gymnastics coach on what was in her lunchbox.

"You've gained weight," she told me out of the blue as I hopped down from a balance beam one day, "What are you eating for lunch? For dinner?"

To reiterate: I was 11. I was supposed to gain weight because that's how children grow.

"I don't know," I shrugged, "Peanut butter, applesauce, pasta." I waited nervously for her reply.

"That's fine," she said dismissively, "Do you eat *a lot* of pasta?"

"Maybe," I replied awkwardly.

"You should try whole wheat spaghetti," she suggested.

"Okay," I mumbled, backing away from the balance beam and wishing I were not there.

After giving my coach a rundown of the contents of my childhood meals, I tried to push her comments from my mind. I was not successful. That conversation has played over and over in my head for the better part of 20 years. The size of my body and the content of my meals would become more and more of an obsession as I transitioned to middle school and high school. By college, my body dysmorphia was spiraling out of control.

My thoughts had been disordered for a long time, but my eating patterns didn't become disordered until the day that I showed up for preseason training and realized that I was the tallest and largest person on the cheerleading team. I may only be 5'6", but college cheerleaders are classically petite.

The day after my first practice, I marched myself to Jimmy John's and ordered a lettuce wrap. There would be no more bread for me—which explains why I never tried the glory that is challah French toast until I was already Jewish. Pizza, fries, burritos, vanilla lattes, and beer were out, too, despite being staples of the Ann Arbor college student diet. From Pizza House, I ordered spinach salads; at Charlie's, I ordered a modest gin and tonic while my classmates shared a "fishbowl." I whittled down my diet until it included only the most depressing essentials: oatmeal, egg whites, salads absent of dressing, chicken and fish, un-salted sweet potato cubes. I counted every calorie and started running for 30 minutes a day. I later upped it to 60. I ran in the rain and snow, and I once ran when I was still tipsy on St. Patricks' Day. The cardio was in addition to cheer practice and the hot yoga sessions that I would attend once or twice a week with sorority sisters. Studying and exercising takes up a lot of energy, so I was still eating enough calories to avoid looking emaciated, but only about half of what my body probably required. I dropped almost 20 pounds in six months, and I didn't believe people when they said I looked different.

Being diagnosed with an eating disorder is only easy if you're so thin that you get sent to the hospital. I was in an unfortunate middle ground: losing weight rapidly, getting ill frequently, but still fed enough to look and act relatively "normal." When my worried athletic trainer sent me to the athletic department physician, I was embarrassed and unwilling to accept help.

"What are you doing?" the doctor demanded. "What's wrong with you?"

"Nothing is wrong with me," I insisted defensively.

"Are you not eating?"

"I eat some things," I said evasively.

"Are you making yourself throw up?" she demanded.

"Rarely," I offered casually. She gave a sigh of irritation.

"It's really not good for you," she scolded.

"I had no idea," I replied sarcastically.

She looked distinctly unamused. After a quick exam, the physician crossed her arms and said that I looked okay. She instructed me to see a psychologist, which I did, but otherwise I interpreted her lack of concern as permission to keep going to bed hungry.

For the blissfully unaware, eating disorders take up a lot of mental space. When you aren't working or studying, you're counting calories, planning exercise routines, lamenting how large you are even after your clothes have started to hang limply on you. All day, food was in the back of my mind. At night, I dreamed about food, usually chocolate. It's a miracle that I was able to stay on top of my grades and athletics. I had to cut out some other luxuries, like dating either of the cute Jewish boys I had a crush on. I bounced from the classroom to practice to sorority events in a bit of a haze. My inability to make room for anything more is probably the reason that I never showed up at Hillel, begging to convert. It would have been too much.

It took me the better part of two years to kick the disordered eating and thinking. It was largely my own sheer force of will that saw me through. I eventually got sick of being run down and hungry all the time, and I vowed to get better. I had to do it on my own time. I started taking therapy more seriously, and I talked to close friends about how they could support me. Ironically, other than therapy, the person who was most helpful to me during recovery was someone I met through the Catholic Church.

After about two years of struggling with my eating and exercise habits, we came to the Christian season of Lent. I was subsisting primarily on egg whites and spinach salads. I was tired. After consulting with a couple of trusted adults, I did the responsible thing and signed up for a therapy slot at the University mental health service. In addition, I signed up to have weekly meetings with a Lenten prayer buddy. My buddy's name was Kelly, and she was and is one of my favorite human beings on the planet. Kelly was beautiful, and she radiated warmth and kindness. Her office in the church annex was filled with light, and she would always pull her chair around her desk so that we could sit across from each other and make proper eye contact. She started each meeting by taking several deep breaths and very softly and quietly asking me to tell her about my week. She was never in a rush, and she didn't pry. She asked questions more than she gave opinions. Her presence was calming; she was a textbook good listener. I would tell Kelly how things were going in therapy, and she would reassure me that I was doing my best and that the situation I was in didn't make me a bad person. I always left her office feeling confident and centered.

Kelly represented the best of what the Church can offer: nonjudgmental fellowship and support through attention and prayer. If not for her, maybe I would have left the Church sooner.

But I did get better, and I did leave the Church. That meant I was on my own to figure out whether recovery and *kashrut* could live in harmony. Living with an eating disorder isn't much of a way to live, after all, and I knew I would never allow myself to be sucked back in if I could prevent it.

* * *

"Our diet is almost kosher, anyway," Travis ventured cautiously. "We have to make a few small tweaks, and if it doesn't work, it doesn't work."

"You're right," I told him. "It shouldn't be that much change. I can do it." I hoped I could, anyway.

The Jewish dietary guidelines were straightforward enough: eat only kosher meat, don't mix meat with dairy, cut out pork and shellfish. I feared that the finer details would force me to think about food more than necessary. (Only eating food with a kosher label, refusing to eat food from non-kosher kitchens, shunning non-kosher wines, waiting a certain number of hours before eating dairy after a meat meal, etc. *Kashrut* can certainly become more of a constraint, depending on the person). The easiest way to keep kosher for a lot of Jews is to keep a vegan or vegetarian diet. I had done reasonably well being a vegetarian before and during part of law school, but I was always flexible with myself and would choose meat over hunger if those were my options. Given that, I decided to incorporate poultry and fish into my kosher diet in order to maximize my options though we often revert to vegetarianism. We're all in process. Always.

The reasons for the rules of *kashrut* vary depending on who you ask. Some rabbis will tell you that they are what they are because God said so—read the Torah and you'll see. Another explanation is that paying attention to what you eat can slow you down and "sanctify" the act of eating; this line of thinking is an argument for saying blessings before and after meals, as well as for observing the laws of *kashrut*. There is also a particular justification for not mixing milk and meat, which is to avoid mixing life (represented by dairy) with death (meat). Judaism tends to provide a panoply of perspectives, which I deeply appreciate.

The explanation that spoke most to me personally was to think about using the laws of *kashrut* to eat more mindfully—to think about food equity, environmental impact, animal rights, food waste, and more. To the extent that my observance connects me to food and other people and the planet that we share in meaningful ways, it is worth the effort. I always tell other potential converts that their observance will be the most joyful and consistent when it speaks to them.

Once I had a plan and sense of what *kashrut* meant to me, it was time to tweak the contents of our kitchen. Cooking at home proved to be easy. Travis and I made a variety of plant-based meals, as well as salmon filets and an array of Italian pizza and pasta staples. When I wanted to increase the variety in our meal planning, I would drive out to the Chicago suburbs to shop at Hungarian Kosher Foods. There, I would find kosher chicken and deli meat, a variety of blintzes and pierogis, and a healthy selection of premade challah.

When I told our cantor that I had been shopping somewhat regularly at Hungarian for kosher chicken and blintzes, she gasped in surprise.

"I don't even shop there!" she exclaimed. "I feel like I'm not religious enough to shop there! I always feel like people have their eye on me."

It occurred to me that I wasn't giving myself enough credit for how bold we were about jumping in. When we started our conversion course, I had never heard of certain holidays like Purim. I couldn't read or write Hebrew. I didn't know what you could do on Shabbat or whether glazed donuts were kosher. And yet here I was, proudly picking out a loaf of challah at a kosher grocery store so that I could log off and enjoy Shabbat with Travis. A few shoppers glanced at us skeptically here and there, but it turns out that my fear of being outright rejected by other Jews was unfounded. No one really cared that I was there as long as I didn't take the last of the good kosher wines.

Keeping kosher while dining out of the house was slightly more restrictive, but I managed. I ate piles of chips and salsa at Uncle Julio's and explored new varieties of kosher sushi. I had to give up Nando's chicken (sadly, not kosher), but I kept buying their pineapple dole whip on hot days. Some Jews won't eat out at all if the restaurant isn't kosher (i.e., doesn't serve any non-kosher foods and the kitchen is under rabbinical supervision). I knew that avoiding non-kosher restaurants was not going to be possible.

"Do some Jews really only eat at kosher restaurants?" I asked my former professor one day over a vegetarian lunch in Ann Arbor. "Are there a lot of those outside of New York?"

"Not really," she admitted, "And some of them aren't very good. You have to really think about what you want your life to look like. It's your decision."

"I'm proud of being Jewish," I explained, "but I certainly don't want to be alienated, especially at work."

"That's fine," she assured me. "I eat vegetarian food at restaurants. There's nothing wrong with how you're doing it."

I nodded appreciatively. Conversion had changed my life quite a bit, and I was anxious to hold on to the ability to eat out with friends and colleagues.

On the day of Travis's law school graduation, his school hosted a post-ceremony reception. The kosher food table consisted of cream cheese sandwiches, raw vegetables, and brownies. I was a little baffled by the limited choices, and so were all of the nice Jewish grandparents who stared skeptically at the kosher options before taking a can of soda and wandering off back into the crowd. At the non-kosher food tables, there were trays of hot, gooey macaroni and cheese. Remembering the advice of friends and family, I filled up a paper plate and ate it without guilt. I had to take things one meal at a time.

Vegetarian options rarely fail me, but there are always exceptions. About two months after changing my diet, I had to take a business trip to Green Bay, Wisconsin. If you're hoping to find kosher food in the Green Bay airport, or in Green Bay generally, I have bad news for you. One of my favorite co-workers, Jenna, was on the trip with me. I'd never had occasion to announce my religious affiliation to her. My law firm wasn't the kind of place where colleagues inquire about your personal life. When we settled in at an airport deli, I glanced uneasily at the menu. It consisted primarily of non-kosher meats and steamed hot dogs.

"I think," I said uneasily, "That I might have to look for somewhere else to eat. I keep kosher and ..." Starting to talk about your delicate new practice always feels a little bit surreal at first, but Judaism is something that you do as much as something you believe, so it's nearly impossible to do it in a way that's completely private.

"It's not a problem," Jenna replied easily. Without batting an eye, she asked the burly man at the deli counter where the other restaurants in the airport were.

"There are no other restaurants," he explained flatly. "There's another deli. Like this deli. Only over there." He pointed vaguely down the hallway.

"Got it," I said slowly. I looked around for a veggie wrap of some sort.

"We're out," the cashier said flatly when I asked about the chances of finding a hummus wrap.

"Are the hot dogs kosher?" I inquired, my hope realistically low. My co-worker waited patiently while the cashier sighed and went to examine the refrigerator. Unsurprisingly, the answer was no. There were a few different bags of chips available, so I resigned myself to eating chips for lunch. The flight home would be short, and I could eat in Chicago.

"Can you have tuna?" my co-worker asked politely, gesturing to a single prewrapped tuna and cheese sandwich that was sitting by itself in a smudged display case.

I quickly racked my brain to remember if you could mix dairy and fish. In fact, I could.

I scooped up the sandwich and paid for it quickly. It tasted terrible, but I felt victorious nonetheless. I apologized to my colleague for having taken so long to settle the sandwich situation.

"Don't apologize," she responded warmly, "I'm really religious, too. I study my Bible all the time. My parents are pastors."

I wanted to hug her. It didn't matter that she was deeply involved in the religion that I'd kicked to the curb.

The first time that you say out loud that you keep kosher can feel like a vulnerable moment. It's intimidating the first time that you turn off your electronics for the Sabbath or take off work on a Jewish holiday. Religious observance in the secular world—at least as a Jew—can be a lonely experience. Having Jenna's ongoing support as I navigated the intricacies of kosher food and Sabbath observance prevented me from scrapping my public observance altogether in those tender, early days of Jewish practice.

I was gentle and flexible with myself, so it turned out that keeping kosher was doable after all. I never struggled with the disordered thoughts that I had feared. After converting, Travis and I went back to keeping a vegetarian home and ordering non-meat entrees at restaurants. Sometimes, Travis sneaks a bowl of clam chowder. Our daughter makes a habit of eating scones and croissants during Passover while Travis and I avoid leavened breads like Jewish law commands. We try to be flexible and make the right choice for the moment. *Kashrut* has had its ups and downs, but I have found it to be a positive addition to my life rather than a stressor. When I say a *bracha*, or blessing, over my meal or alter a recipe to comport with *kashrut*, it's a reminder that I have the power to turn something as routine as eating into something more meaningful. Food doesn't have power over me; it's the other way around.

CHAPTER 13

"Ask about your neighbors, then buy the house."
–*Jewish proverb*

Because I was hoping to make my conversion a one-year affair instead of two or more years, I signed up for an additional conversion course that would take place on Tuesday evenings. The overachiever was back at it.

The second program was at Mishkan, an exciting Jewish community on the north side of Chicago. Mishkan, true to its name, is a "traveling sanctuary" that takes their services to assorted spots around Chicago. Worship might be set up formally in the gymnasium of another synagogue, or it might make its way to a historic Chicago theater or even into the living room of a community member's home. Mishkan describes itself as "inspired, down to earth" Judaism. The community is radically inclusive, and services manage to create the kind of fun that my old evangelical church was after without all of the fundamentalism lurking underneath. Conversion courses were held in their home office, which featured a concrete bunker-style classroom, tastefully decorated with colorful rugs and a lot of books. When we arrived for Tuesday night classes, there would be a wine and cheese table ready to welcome us and put us at ease.

The conversion program involved a lot of the same learning: Jewish belief, holidays, basic Hebrew, and a little history. At Mishkan, though, the rabbinical staff focused more on feelings around conversion: fear, longing, and belonging. Anshe Emet was primarily an intellectual encounter while Mishkan focused on the emotional dimensions of conversion. My cohort at Mishkan showed up with heavy-hitting questions about whether Judaism had a place for disabled Jews, queer Jews, interfaith families, and doubting atheists. Our rabbis, Jeff and Ally, rose to the occasion week after week. They taught me about a living Judaism, the kind that embraces change without straying from the community's core values. They spoke passionately of an ancient, humble tradition that rises up to meet the needs of today's practicing Jews with a combination of wisdom from our elders and deep respect for the ways in which Jews and their communities change over time. Judaism isn't perfect, but it felt like everyone could have a home in it.

Things weren't always easy. One cohort member was losing the support of his family for leaving Christianity and embracing Judaism. Another new friend was going to have to give up a career in a Christian ministry space to become a Jew. One very enthusiastic convert shared with us that his wife was disappointed that he was getting "too into Judaism." She wanted him to convert, sure, but not with so much gusto. Watching him take her tradition and make it his own was confusing and surprisingly painful for her. Another classmate felt like she didn't want to convert at all but that her in-laws would never accept her if she didn't.

"I don't know if I want to convert when this course is over," one woman reminded us every week while her Jewish wife nodded kindly in support. "But I like what I'm hearing."

It was remarkable, the long and difficult journeys that brought all of our souls to the same table every Tuesday night. More remarkable still was the way that Judaism made a place for us without ever being pushy or demanding. Judaism doesn't hurry. There were no simple solutions to all of these tough situations, and Judaism didn't purport to find them. We gave each other the gift of good, empathetic listening, and that had to be enough.

In addition to all of the emotional and spiritual work that we did at Mishkan, there was plenty of room for joy. Mishkan hosts inspiring Friday night Shabbat services and holiday events. The first time I attended Mishkan's Friday night service and potluck, chairs arranged in a circle around Rabbi Lizzi on her guitar, I was mesmerized. Rabbi Lizzi beautifully makes Hebrew prayers accessible to beginners while providing a rich prayer and study experience for lifelong Jews, as well.

One Friday night, in the darkness of an auditorium with 100 or so Jews surrounding me, I swayed to her music and felt like I was finally at home. We worshipped to beautiful music, and Rabbi Jeff gave a stinging sermon on toxic masculinity in the media. When services were over, we gathered to enjoy a vegetarian potluck dinner and chat about everything from politics to prayer to the best recipe for *cholent*, which I learned was an Ashkenazi stew of sorts.

Services were inspiring, and the Purim party that Mishkan threw during the year of my conversion was a riot. Although Purim celebrates a very serious thing, i.e. escaping genocide, the holiday is celebrated in a decidedly non-serious way, with costumes and cookies, causing a general ruckus during the *megillah* reading. We enjoyed the family-friendly Purim carnival at Anshe Emet, but we also wanted to make sure that we went to an adult-focused *megillah* reading, where the scroll of Esther is recited. Travis and I did actually find costumes for the Mishkan party (though mine was more like pajamas) and took half a day off work to allow ample time for Purim festivities. Mishkan's party involved a spirited *megillah* reading and a wild dance party that went into the wee morning hours of the next workday.

To be clear, the *megillah* is a sacred text. We honor the text by stomping our feet and cranking our noisemakers when we hear the name of Haman, the genocidal enemy, and cheering when we hear the name of one of the protagonists, Mordechai. (The other protagonist, of course, is Esther, after whom the scroll of Esther is named).

I loved my noisemaker, called a *grogger*. I loved that it was to be unabashedly shaken during what is otherwise a fairly serious scripture reading. I couldn't believe that I was allowed to yell "boo" when a bad actor was being quoted in scripture. I also couldn't get enough of the oversized, fluffy apricot *hamentaschen* that Mishkan had stuffed in our goodie bags, even more so given that I was allowed to munch on my cookie during services. Christmas is fun, sure, but I was dressed up like the genie from *Aladdin* and drinking themed cocktails on a Tuesday night and calling it a religious holiday. This was what dreams are made of. My spirits were only partially dampened by the constant patrol of security officers.

"What are they doing here?" I asked Travis as I munched on a slice of kosher pizza, voice still hoarse from cheering for Mordechai during the *megillah* reading.

"You know what they're doing here," he said sadly. "Making sure we don't get attacked for having the audacity to be loudly Jewish on Purim."

The reality that I was suddenly part of an event that might be targeted by a hateful shooter was a tough one to swallow. Nothing had changed about me in the past year except for my religion, and yet, every time I took myself to a Jewish space, my safety was potentially in danger. There were people who didn't hate me yesterday who would hate me today. Antisemitism is strange because it treats Judaism like something you *are* instead of something that you *do*. And maybe that's the case. There are plenty of Jewish people who don't practice, just like there are plenty of practicing Jews who you couldn't identify as such based on outdated and unfounded notions of who looks like a Jew. It was all part of navigating the difference between joining a religion and joining a culture.

Because Judaism has ethnic components, I sometimes felt self-conscious that Jews would accuse me of "stealing their heritage." In my first one-on-one meeting with Rabbi Ally at Mishkan, I confessed that I was more nervous about what other Jews would think about my conversion than fellow Christians.

"Judaism is something that is passed down from generation to generation whether the adherents are religious or not," I explained. "Won't Jews feel like I'm stealing something that doesn't belong to me?"

Rabbi Ally thought carefully about my question. Like always, she approached her answer with a great deal of care.

"Imagine this," she explained, "You grow up Jewish, going to Hebrew school and celebrating holidays with your families. There is a little joy, but mostly a lot of 'oy.' You don't really value your Jewish heritage; you don't think much of it at all. Then, someone comes along, an acquaintance who was not raised Jewish, and they tell you that they saw so much value in your tradition that they decided to take that tradition for themselves. How surreal must it feel to watch somebody discover the beauty of a tradition that you viewed as a burden?"

I took some time to digest her perspective. People would not be mad at me for "stealing" their tradition, but it might bring up baggage surrounding their own relationship to Judaism or their Jewish education. In so many things, our reactions to what goes on in other peoples' lives is simply a reflection of how we feel about our own life. It's always about us and rarely about them.

My conversation with Rabbi Ally inspired me to reach out to my Jewish contacts and let them know about the conversion. I didn't owe any of them an explanation or a head's up, but I wanted to give them a chance to be happy for me as much as I wanted to give them a chance to feel confused or annoyed or threatened. As it would happen, none of them felt anything other than joy.

I tested the waters by dropping the news to my friend and colleague Carolyn by inviting her out to dinner for latkes and blintzes during Hanukkah. I had intended to tell her that Travis and I were converting to Judaism and that we would love to take her out for a meal during Hanukkah since she couldn't make it home to see her family. What I actually did was corner her during our firm's annual trial training exercise and ask her, "Hey, there's this really great hole in the wall on Division Street that serves latkes, would you like to go next Tuesday during Hanukkah?"

"I would love to," Carolyn replied. There was a long, uneasy silence as we walked toward the business center of the Chicago Marriott to print our cross-examination outlines. Carolyn might be the politest human being on the planet, and I could tell that she was choosing her next words with care. "The only thing," she added, as polite as ever, "is that I didn't realize that either of you were Jewish."

"We're converting," I said quickly, getting it out before I could change my mind.

"Oh!" she exclaimed, taking in the big news that I had so tactlessly delivered, "Well, I'm so happy for you. That's amazing. I can't wait to hear all about it."

That was it. No demanding questions. No taking offense to me running off with her heritage. She was unabashedly happy for me, and if she was baffled, she hid it well.

"Yeah, I guess I haven't told many people," I sighed with relief. "It's not, like, a secret."

"I understand," she said breezily, organizing her cross-exam outline as she spoke. "I won't say anything to anyone."

"Okay," I smiled, "I'll get around to telling the masses," I promised, stapling my own outline and smoothing my Ann Taylor dress.

"You don't owe them anything," she reminded me. I nodded appreciatively and felt myself relax a bit. No thanks to me, my first unplanned "I'm converting" conversation had gone remarkably well. Emboldened by my success, I reached out to a few other Jewish acquaintances. I kept the circle small: a couple of old college friends and my former clinical law professor. For the most part, I kept the conversion under wraps. I wasn't ashamed, but I wasn't ready to hear everyone's opinions on my own religious journey. My newfound faith felt delicate and private, and I wanted to keep it to myself for a while longer.

Having more Jews in my corner made it easier for me to navigate my unfamiliar new world. I ran my questions about Jewish culture past Alana and Carolyn. I asked them how to make non-soggy latkes (Alana says to save yourself the trouble and buy some from Trader Joe's) and what to wear to certain holiday services (something trendy yet modest). They sometimes gave two very different answers, which was both confusing and delightfully Jewish.

When Travis's former boss, Rep. John Dingell, passed away, I grilled Carolyn on the laws of *shiva*.

"Can you only sit *shiva* for parents and spouses?" I asked her. "Because Travis is really distraught. They had a very close relationship. I want to light the candle for him."

"Go buy a *shiva* candle!" she replied immediately, "Don't overthink it."

"We only have a *Yartzeit* candle," I moaned.

"Just light the candle," she assured me. "Stop worrying. May his memory be a blessing."

It meant a lot to me to have another Jew's blessing as we tried to figure out how it all worked. For the most part, our friends encouraged us to do what felt right when we were unclear on a point of Jewish practice. I often ask my rabbi what is customary; sometimes I ask friends, not infrequently I turn to Google; and other times I just use my gut.

As our practice came together, I started wondering whether other people could see my Jewish-ness on me. I felt different, but I dressed the same and talked the same. On a weekend trip to New York City for work, Travis and I woke up early and walked to Williamsburg from our Airbnb in Clinton Hill to get breakfast at a shop with its kosher certification displayed on the window. The shop was tiny and was attended by two observant Jews with sidelocks and long black coats. I smiled at them broadly while we ordered bagels with smoked salmon as if to say *I'm one of you.*

"Good morning!" I chirped, "*Shavua Tov!*" They looked surprised at my Hebrew but gave the salutation back to me. Our practices might differ, but we're all Jews.

"It's better with red onion. The bagel and lox ..." one of the men said, gesturing to my bagel with a small smile.

"Thanks for the tip," I replied, smiling back.

As Travis and I settled in to eat our breakfast, suitcases at our feet, I watched people walk up and down the street outside. Men heading to services with their prayer books, women with baby carriages and long black skirts.

"They're not actually going to consider us Jewish," Travis pointed out sadly. "Our conversion isn't Orthodox."

"It's okay," I said reassuringly. "We don't have to convince everyone that we're Jewish enough. Let's just be Jewish."

"I guess," Travis conceded, sinking his teeth into his bagel.

"We belong," I said firmly. "It's okay if their Judaism looks different. Ours is still real."

"I know," Travis replied, wiping some stray cream cheese from his mouth. He sounded more certain this time.

CHAPTER 14

Ask two Jews, get three opinions.

I said this wouldn't be a theology book, and I meant it. On the other hand, it is impossible to understand why I would convert to Judaism without understanding which Jewish ideas started to fill in the cracks that my previous religion left behind.

You don't need religion at all, as so many friends advised me. This is true: you can be a happy, ethical person with no involvement in organized religion. If not for Judaism, I might have listened to them and moved on. Instead, I found in Judaism such sensible, beautiful ideas that I believe this story warrants a brief interlude about some of the most compelling things I learned over the course of my time studying. With no agenda as to earning your agreement on the "correctness" of any of these ideas, here are the ones that pulled me in and embraced me with their wisdom. Take all of them with a grain of salt. Different groups of Jews believe vastly different things, and Jewish theology is infinitely complex.

1. I was drawn to Judaism because it is a non-evangelizing religion by nature.

Judaism is a covenant; it represents a promise between God and the people of Israel. Jews presume that non-Jews will not abide by most of that covenant; it wouldn't make sense for them to. Most movements of mainstream Christianity, on the other hand, posit that everyone must put their faith in Christ in order to have eternal salvation. Even more, it's important that believers go out and spread Christianity in order to make more Christians.

Jews are not supposed to go out and seek converts. In this vein, most movements of Judaism don't focus on whether Judaism is the "right" tradition for everyone—it's the tradition that belongs to the Jews. In my experience, other Jews were consistently enthusiastic about my conversion, but it was always clear that I had sought out conversion on my own. Judaism's neutrality about my membership in the community was a relief rather than an offense.

A lot of non-Jews assume that my conversion classes focused on why Judaism was better or more correct than other religions. That is not the case. The cantors and rabbis that I worked with presented Jewish ideas as they are without advancing a view of their supremacy. No one spoke ill of Christianity because we didn't speak about Christianity at all. Judaism is a world unto itself.

The permission to believe in something without asking other people to adopt my beliefs was a seismic shift from my Catholic youth group days. I looked forward to having faith without needing to spread it.

From my perspective, it's hard to conduct evangelization in a way that respects the boundaries of potential converts and advances a neutral view of religion rather than a supremacist view of the tradition being peddled.

I have met a number of people over the years who were happy to have found Christianity and found great healing and purpose in the Christian tradition. This is wonderful. Unfortunately, I've met even more people who felt harassed and violated by aggressive proselytization. One of my peers in law school shared with me that she felt exhausted by her friends' well-meaning insistence that she was going to hell if she didn't accept the Christian faith. They believed that it was their Christian duty to save her soul at all costs while she believed that hell was a pernicious myth and wished to be respected in her nonbelief. Believers and nonbelievers are in a constant state of impasse like this. To be a good Christian, you must spread the message of Christ. To be true to yourself as an atheist, you must constantly reject it. This is an exhausting cycle. When I converted to Judaism, I could leave that tension behind. I was a Jew. It didn't matter whether my acquaintances were not.

2. I was drawn to Judaism because I appreciated its teachings regarding mourning and death.

During my time here on earth, I have lost two of my very favorite family members. I lost my cousin Matthew suddenly and unexpectedly to a plane crash, and I lost my maternal grandmother to old age after a long battle with dementia. In both instances, I turned to my faith to cope with the harsh realities of loss. Despite my best intentions,

I always found myself feeling disquieted by the notion that I should rejoice in my ability to see my loved ones "on the other side," which is an idea that comes up frequently in Christian spaces. In my experience, that idea has not come up in Jewish spaces, at least not in interpersonal conversations surrounding loss.

To advance the view that death is not a final goodbye, you have to believe that the afterlife looks something like a movie: we all meet our loved ones in heaven and "hang out." I was sixteen when my cousin passed away. I didn't want to imagine dying and hanging out in heaven; I wanted to live with my cousin still beside me. As I had no siblings, he was one of my closest confidants. As appealing as the Christian afterlife sounded, I needed him with me on earth to play cards and gossip about mean teachers. In my grandmother's instance, we were ready to let her go after her long battle with dementia, but the next several years of my life were informed by her acute absence from the realm of the living. I wanted her to attend my law school graduation and to hold my daughter at the hospital, marveling over her sparkling blue eyes. The fact that she couldn't physically be there for those moments felt tragic, no matter what the priest said about "better places" and reuniting in the afterlife.

My grandmother was blessed with a long and mostly happy life that was drawn out by disease and decline at the end; my cousin's life had been cut short artificially when he was young and engaged to be married. I'm not sure whether there was a "right time" for either of them to go. It was what it was, and it was hard. I missed them both terribly and still do.

Christian messaging around death leans a little too hard into the concept of hope and comfort, so it never fully resonated with me. As long as I was stuck on earth chugging along, I wanted my loved ones to be here with me. I think that this is the reality of death: that no matter what we tell ourselves, the pain of living without the person we loved can feel unbearable and to pretend otherwise is disingenuous.

I found solace in Judaism's practical approach to the difficulties of saying goodbye. Though Jewish thinking on death and afterlife is complex, my conversion program at Anshe Emet mostly focused on grief and the logistics of mourning. Jews treat the dead with great care and arrange a speedy, dignified send-off. It is a tradition for family members to tear their clothing, or tear a ribbon, at the burial as a gesture of grief. That felt about right to me. We then turn our focus to mourners, surrounding them with company and donated meals. Instead of "you'll see them again," Jews often say "may their memory be a blessing." When I read a guide to comforting Jewish mourners in the days following the loss of a loved one, it emphasized that it is not necessary to say or do anything specific. It emphasized that the gift of your presence is enough. The guide suggested prompting the mourner to share happy memories of their loved one rather than trying to console them with platitudes. That sounded wise to me.

"There are stages of grief that Jewish teaching recognizes," an Orthodox rabbi once explained to me and

Travis at a casual meeting. "The first 24 hours following a death involves a lot of numbness, so mourners are excused from some of the obligations of Jewish life. The next week is for grieving at home during *shiva*, while the entire month following the loss is still recognized as a period of grieving even as the mourner returns to their daily routine." That timeline sounded about right based on my own experiences with loss.

3. I was drawn to Judaism because it reminded me that our life on earth is something to be cherished.

I first encountered the concept of *pikuach nefesh* when one of my fellow Jewish community members explained that she keeps her phone on during Shabbat services despite the usual prohibition on technology. *Pikuach nefesh* means that preserving human life overrides almost any other Jewish law.

"I'm a foster parent," my new friend explained. "Any call could involve the well-being of a child, so I answer my phone on Shabbat, even at services."

Liz reiterated the concept in our classes. *Pikauch nefesh* is why some pregnant women eat on Yom Kippur and why we can drive to the hospital on Shabbat. It is why many synagogues close during health or safety crises and why abortions are permitted to preserve the health of the pregnant person. It is why Jews are frequently urged to follow medical advice on vaccines and to pursue life-saving treatment whenever possible.

In Christianity, I often encountered the idea that the earth is merely a waystation on our journey to heaven. Life matters, sure, but only to an extent. I encountered that idea less often in Judaism. Our lives on earth are valuable and important, so we do whatever we can to protect them. Christians often talk about our bodies being temples, but that verse was only quoted to me when we were being told not to have sex or wear slutty clothing. There wasn't a push to vaccinate the temple of our body, so to speak.

Judaism's message is fairly consistent: life is a gift, and it's something worth sticking around for. I take care to remember this even in the moments when life doesn't feel so rosy.

4. I was drawn to Judaism because you really can't beat Shabbat.

I was—and still am at the time of writing this book—a lawyer in the corporate world. When I heard that the Sabbath involves approximately 25 hours of putting down one's work, I was convinced that it wasn't going to be possible. Lawyers take pride in working all the time. Our lives revolve around the constant buzz of our inboxes. Anything a client needs could rightfully be called an emergency as long as the definition of emergency is stretched and distorted to include commercial loss. Doing it now is always better than doing it later in the mind of most lawyers. Being absent for 24 hours is unthinkable.

I could have become Jewish and continued to work for my law firm on Shabbat. We no longer stone people for breaking the Sabbath. Regardless, Jewish observance does not require you to fear retribution in order to connect with a community tradition. The Sabbath has become a treasured part of my family's Jewish life not because I fear God's wrath if I don't observe but because I want to observe it. Every Friday at sundown, I bill my time for the week and shut down my computer. If a client calls, they won't be hearing from me until nightfall on Saturday. I still do more than enough work to get by.

The Sabbath has been a crash course in the concept of "enough." I don't buy things on the Sabbath because it is a day to recognize that we *have enough*. I don't work on the Sabbath because it is a day to recognize that we *do enough*. I don't gossip about other people on the Sabbath because it's a day to recognize that those people *are enough* (though we shouldn't gossip on other days either— still working on that). On the Sabbath, I take a break from creating in order to see that what has been created already is good. I take a break from this restless existence to acknowledge that rest is required. Whatever troubles existed at sundown on Friday will greet me at sundown on Saturday. Everyone likes to feel important, but there is freedom in realizing that the outside world will not burn if you turn inward for a day.

5. I was drawn to Judaism because of its sense of community.

When I was a teenager, I had a friend whose family somewhat jokingly called good deeds "HPs" for Heaven Points. When one of us would clean up the kitchen or volunteer for a community service event, we would exclaim, "Getting those HPs!"

In all of my time as a practicing Jew, no rabbi or Jewish scholar has ever suggested that I should do anything for the sake of bettering my experience in the afterlife. This is largely because Jews don't picture ourselves standing in a single file line at heaven's gates being judged on our earthly behavior. Instead, there is a belief that God will look at the Jewish community as one people. Even if I don't take this idea literally, there is beauty in the emphasis on community. We can fill in for each other's weaknesses rather than spending our lives trying to pray our weaknesses away. In this sense, we can save one another from our faults. We can speak kindly when someone else gossips or give when someone else hoards. I have always felt that the Jewish community is more tight-knit and welcoming than other communities that I have been a part of, and I treasure the opportunity to make connections with people even if the only thing we share is Judaism.

6. *I was drawn to Judaism because of its perspective on sin and forgiveness.*

When I read about the Hebrew definition of sin, I was blown away. To sin means to shoot an arrow and miss the target. You goofed up, as we often do. To the extent that there is *yetzer hara* (the inclination toward evil), there is also *yetzer hatov* (the inclination to goodness). Judaism encourages us to reconcile with those we have harmed before turning to the divine for forgiveness. A Jewish apology involves recognizing that we caused harm, expressing genuine remorse, and then ensuring that we don't make the same mistake again. Notably absent from this formula is making an excuse or minimizing the harm. The process is called *tshuva*, or "to return." The concept is so simple, but it has never failed me in practice.

When I was pregnant, I was suffering from persistent insomnia. I was tired all the time, and the exhaustion mimicked symptoms of depression. I would curl up in bed during the day, my laptop glowing beside me, and alternate among working, crying, and napping. I felt so crappy that I dropped the ball a few times on a case that I cared a lot about. When you drop the ball at work, someone else generally has to pick it up. My colleague Christina, who was already quite busy, stepped up and moved the case along. I could have told Christina that I was struggling, but I was too proud. My pride harmed her because she was left to do my work without any clue as to what was going on.

When I returned from maternity leave, I asked her to call me so that I could apologize. She was surprised but acquiesced. I gathered my courage and told her that I was sorry that I hadn't been a good teammate. I told her that I knew it must have made her feel disrespected and that she had to spend her valuable time filling in for me. I told her that it wouldn't happen again, and I outlined what I was going to do that week to keep the case moving forward. I didn't whine about prenatal depression or bring up how helpful I had been since returning from leave. I gave her a true apology and told her that she didn't need to feel pressured to forgive me. I was going to do better either way. When we offer someone this kind of apology—given without excuses and with real feeling—both we and the person we harmed can move toward forgiveness. It was the most *halachically* Jewish apology I ever made.

In Jewish spaces, we have spent a lot more time talking about how to repair our own wrongs than we have spent talking about our responsibility to forgive. Of course, forgiveness is an ideal path forward for both parties, but Judaism is less likely to demand it indiscriminately. The power of choice is a gift. If I ask for forgiveness three times and the person I harmed still withholds it, I am allowed to forgive myself and move forward. Luckily, if your apology is genuine, one usually does the trick.

7. I was drawn to Judaism because I enjoy wrestling with the concept of tikkun olam.

I hesitate to go too deeply into the theology of *tikkun olam* because its historical meaning is quite different from how modern Jews think about it. But if one of my gripes with Catholicism was that community service made me feel a bit like I was spinning my wheels, there is at least some version of *tikkun olam* that spoke to what was missing.

I had great conversations with many rabbis about what makes *tikkun olam* special. Liz Berke at Anshe Emet emphasized that Jews don't perform *tikkun olam* with any expectations. We don't necessarily do it to show people the love of God, in the hopes of winning converts, or in order to perform "good works" that earn favor in the afterlife. When something is broken, we must fix it. Rabbi Rubenstein from Congregation Beth Ahm somewhat disagrees, pointing out that Judaism recognizes that good deeds on earth also sanctify God's name and bring attention to God's character. I can appreciate the tension.

Rabbi Lizzi Heydemann from Mishkan emphasized that *tikkun olam* means to heal the world, not to put a Band-Aid on a problem. This explains Mishkan's mission to organize Jews to be involved politically; you should not volunteer to paint an elementary school on Monday and vote not to fund it on Tuesday. Catholics were also interested in organizing voting around issues like abortion (though, often, voting for a candidate who will end abortion necessarily means voting for a candidate who refuses to curb gun violence).

I simply felt more at home with the Jewish model of good deeds. We heal the world because that work must be done, and we don't expect anything out of the bargain. Rabbi Lizzi helped me to understand that we should feed the hungry but also strive to eliminate hunger and poverty systemically. My clinical professor Debra Chopp would agree—our first reading assignment before serving clients in poverty was to think about the difference between pulling drowning children out of a river versus marching upstream to find out who keeps throwing them in. We always have to think bigger. I think this is where the concept of service to the world took off for me. I don't claim to be a *tikkun olam* expert, but I have connected deeply with the concept, at least as I have encountered it.

8. I was drawn to Judaism because of the idea that we can wrestle with God and that we can act as God's partners in creation.

Israel means to wrestle with God. Torah study frequently emphasizes Jewish figures who argued with God and challenged God. Some of my Jewish teachers emphasized that God had as much to learn about humans throughout early human history as humans had to learn about the divine. A local Chabad rabbi once sent me a quote that "Torah is God pondering Godself." This two-way partnership was new to me, as was the idea that God would have to continue to *learn* about humanity after creating it. Not only that, but God and I could learn about me together. It was up to me what kind of person I would create, hand-in-hand with the divine, rather than accepting that God had a pre-ordained plan for me.

I was drawn in by all of these beliefs even if they vary greatly across different movements of Judaism. Jews might disagree on any number of theological issues, but diversity of belief was something that interested me more than it confused me. I could let Jewish values speak to me even if I still had questions about the origins of the Torah and of the universe itself.

Jewish values continue to speak to me and guide my family into a life of reflection, meaning, and connection. I didn't have to become a Jew to adopt these teachings as my own, but I am grateful that I did.

CHAPTER 15

"The soul is healed by being with children."
–*Fyodor Dostoyevsky*

In any culture, children are a blessing. To the Jewish community, after facing centuries of suppression and extermination, children are a particular source of hope and joy. When our conversion class attended the Friday night service at Temple Sholom in Chicago, the rabbi leading services hoisted a guitar over her shoulder and invited the children of the congregation up to say *Kiddush*, a prayer of thanks for the bread and wine. Nearly 40 children clamored out of their seats and made their way, pushing and shoving, to the *bimah* at the front of the sanctuary.

Whispering excitedly and tripping over one another, they each took a small cup of grape juice and crowded around the rabbi as she began to strum her guitar. As the prayer started, more children came stomping loudly down the aisles, while other children decided that they would rather run laps around the synagogue. Grape juice was splashing out of tiny cups, and the rabbi's prayer was partially drowned out by raucous laughter. It was barely controlled chaos.

I looked subtly around to gauge the reaction of the congregation. I have never seen so many smiling faces. Some of the older congregation members had lived in countries that disallowed Jewish worship; some of them had felt unsafe to be loudly, visibly Jewish at some point in time. Some might still feel afraid. For the Jewish community, a gaggle of Jewish children proudly raising tiny cups of grape juice during Shabbat evening prayers is a dream come to fruition. The noise was giving me a headache, but I teared up, anyway. I wanted a child. More specifically, I wanted to raise a Jewish child.

We found out that we were pregnant with our third baby, our daughter, on a Monday night shortly after our trip to Temple Sholom. I was at one of our Monday night conversion courses when the idea struck me that I might be pregnant. When I arrived fashionably late to class at 7:05 p.m., I started walking past the open door of our classroom toward the restrooms in the back of the synagogue. Something stopped me.

I shouldn't pee until I get home, I told myself. I should wait and take a pregnancy test tonight.

This wasn't a very rational decision. For one, my period was four or five days away, to the best of my knowledge, so I wouldn't expect to get an accurate result this early. Second, holding your urine is uncomfortable and rarely worth the trouble.

For those of you who haven't been so eager to get pregnant that you change your urination schedule in order to increase your chances of getting an early positive, I'll explain myself a bit. Mommy blog wisdom (and maybe science?) dictates that the best time to take a pregnancy test is first thing in the morning. Presumably, you haven't peed for a while, so any hypothetical trace of HCG in your urine—the hormone indicating pregnancy—should show up. As an alternative, some (probably bonkers) websites suggested that your pregnancy test could be more accurate later in the day if you can manage to hold your urine for four hours before taking a test. Travis generally disapproved of this strategy and insisted that if I could wait until the first day of my missed period like a normal person, we wouldn't have to waste our time and money trying to outsmart biology.

I didn't listen.

It is telling that I don't have the faintest recollection of what that night's topic was. I couldn't focus because, as discussed, I had to pee. After the world's longest class and a short trip home on the CTA Red Line, I slipped into our bathroom and pulled out a First Response test. I worked quietly so that Travis wouldn't complain about me wasting yet another pregnancy test well before my period was expected. Before I had even finished washing my hands, there it was. A faint second pink line on the screen of the test. My heart thudded wildly in my chest. *Stay calm*, I warned myself, *don't get your hopes up*. I walked out of the bathroom expressionless, holding the test out to Travis.

"There's a baby in there," I said softly. "We have another baby."

"Okay," Travis said with a weak, guarded smile. He knew the routine. There were no guarantees.

For the next four weeks, we worked, we watched TV, we went on slow, meandering jogs in Lincoln Park. I flew to New York for the FASPE reunion with my mom and drank a ridiculous amount of ginger ale. We kept attending our conversion classes. We told no one the news.

When we went in for our eight-week ultrasound, I could tell that my doctor was as anxious as we were. I don't think I took a breath while my doctor prepared the ultrasound. I watched her spread cold blue goop on the ultrasound wand and looked at the ceiling lights, willing this baby to be alive. Everything was tense.

"The baby is totally normal," my doctor told me, eyes glued to the monitor beside me. "There's the heartbeat. The measurements are perfect. Congratulations."

Every muscle in my body relaxed. This was amazing news. We were relieved, but we stayed on guard. We weren't out of the woods yet.

We had started our conversion classes in early January, but it was already spring and time for Passover. I couldn't believe how fast four months had gone by. Passover and Easter typically overlap. Easter celebrates the death and resurrection of Jesus, while Passover celebrates the exodus of the Jews from Egypt. Two different stories, but both bring about a sense of hope right in time for spring. Seders are basically festive meals combined with discussing and retelling the story of the exodus of the Jews from Egypt, the commemoration of the Ten Plagues, and a discussion about how the story relates to modern concepts in Jewish life. The seder as we know it today was developed after Jesus' death, so contrary to popular belief, the seders we have today were not part of Jesus' Jewish life.

We were supposed to spend the first Passover seder with one of the rabbis at Anshe Emet and his wife. She was also pregnant but was apparently not constantly curled around a trashcan the way that I was. Since Passover seders are *long*, we opted to stay home.

"Can I eat this?" Travis kept asking from the kitchen. "Is it kosher for Passover?"

"I don't know," I would groan back, popping another grape into my mouth, "Google it."

"Can you use the Internet on the first night of Passover?" he asked back.

"Just Google—oh, I see the problem here."

We both laughed. In the end, Travis settled for tortilla chips and salsa, not knowing whether corn was permitted or not, but preferring not to go hungry in the name of righteousness.

Prior to Passover, I had been living on bagels and cheese pizza. Since neither were kosher for Passover, I turned to hard-boiled eggs, matzoh, and chicken broth. I had purchased an expensive Passover cookbook full of fancy meal ideas and decadent *chametz*-free desserts (*chametz* = leavened grains that are forbidden during Passover), but I didn't have the desire or energy to cook anything. It was anticlimactic.

I thought back to the matzoh pizzas that I had made with my Jewish friend back in college. The whole thing had seemed so complex back then. Now, living out the rules as best as I could in my condition, it felt familiar, as if the tradition had always belonged to me. I liked it, nausea or not.

Passover ended, and we headed back to my obstetrician's office for our twelve-week ultrasound. Travis held my hand, and the ultrasonographer put the dreaded ultrasound wand over my abdomen. There she was, our healthy girl, waving and bouncing.

"*Baruch Hashem*," I whispered, "There she is." Travis cried.

We had made it to the coveted second trimester. We had our baby at last. Watching my daughter float around, perfectly proportioned with a strong heartbeat, I could not doubt that a God existed. The moment was too magical to be purely scientific.

Our lives in Chicago had gotten remarkably comfortable. We had friends at Anshe Emet and Mishkan. Things were going smoothly for me at work, and I had finally stopped feeling queasy around the clock. But spring is a time of change, as they say, and things were changing for us in a major way.

After Pesach, it became clear that we were going to have to move back to Michigan for Travis's job. We had known it was coming for a while, but it was a difficult transition under the circumstances. I cried saying goodbye to my fancy 38th floor office at my law firm, and I cried harder after saying goodbye to my obstetrician. I had grown attached to eating lunch on the floor of my office, staring down at the Chicago River, and I had grown even more attached to my doctor, who had seen us through the past year with remarkable steadiness. I nearly cried saying goodbye to Liz, but I held it together thanks to her ever-calm demeanor. Before leaving for Michigan, Liz and I took a long, meandering walk from the synagogue to Wrigley Field, enjoying the unseasonably warm spring weather.

"I'm going to call you for a pep talk before my *beit din*," I assured her.

"Of course," she said, "You can always call. But you're going to be fine. You two will be wonderful parents and wonderful Jews."

"Thank you," I told her sincerely. "It means a lot. You should call the rabbi in Michigan who's finishing our conversions and tell him how great we are."

"He'll find out for himself," Liz promised. We were very diligent conversion students, so I believed her.

I had actually reached out to a small handful of rabbis in Michigan to see if any of them would take us on as conversion students in order to complete the process. I couldn't find a formal conversion course like the ones that were common in Chicago, so we would have to make more of a one-on-one arrangement. Before converting, I had read more than once that rabbis are bound to ignore or deny potential converts three times to test their sincerity though it has never happened to someone I know personally. Even though I was already in the process of converting, I was worried about being rejected. In order to hedge my bets, I reached out to three rabbis at Conservative synagogues within driving distance of our new house. All three of them had called me back before lunch on the same day I'd reached out. I was amazed and grateful.

I was a little overwhelmed by my options, but I went with my gut. I chose Rabbi Steven Rubenstein, who was affiliated with a fairly small but active congregation near Detroit. He was warm, curious, and enthusiastic. He was temporarily tripped up by the fact that neither of us were converting for marriage, but the fact that we had come to Judaism on our own only cemented his willingness to help. I hated to leave Anshe Emet and Liz, but I sensed that we would develop a wonderful relationship with Rabbi Rubenstein, too.

We left Chicago in May in our densely packed U-Haul, our pet rabbit and developing daughter in tow. It was so cold when I moved into our house in Michigan that I had to wear a hooded sweater with a windbreaker on top.

"Is there an award for having moved the most times between Michigan and Chicago?" Travis grumbled as he tried to wrestle our futon out of the U-Haul.

He was right. We did seem to bounce between Michigan and Chicago every year or so.

"This is the last move," I assured him as I tried to find our plates and forks among the many cardboard boxes we had yet to unload. That was untrue, but I didn't know it yet.

We spent the first couple of weeks back in Michigan unpacking and setting up my home office. By mid-May, we were ready to resume our studies. I sent Rabbi Rubenstein an email and we set up a time to meet in person. The first time we met with him in his cozy office, books stacked from floor to ceiling on his sizable bookshelf, I knew that we had made the right decision, no matter how much it had pained me to leave behind our life in Chicago. Rabbi Rubenstein was insightful and funny.

"Neither of your families are Jewish?" he clarified, his brow furrowed in obvious amusement.

"My brother-in-law's father was a Holocaust survivor, but I never met him, so we can set the Jewish family member count at zero," I replied.

"Do your families know you're converting to Judaism?"

"We told them, of course," I assured him. "My mom doesn't fancy talking about it, but she's aware that it's in the works."

"Okay," he said slowly, "Might it be worth another conversation before we start talking about making a date for the *mikveh*?"

"Nope," I said.

"Ok, thought I'd ask," he said. "And your families are Christian?"

"My parents are Christian by societal default," Travis explained, "but not religious."

"I see," said Rabbi Rubenstein thoughtfully.

"My parents are also not religious to the very best of my knowledge, but my biological mother asked for me to be raised Catholic, which I think is why I spent the first twelve or thirteen years of my life going to Mass against my will." I placed both of my hands over my pregnant belly and leaned back in my chair, waiting for his response.

"If your birth mother is Catholic, is that potentially a reason for you to stay Catholic?" he asked lightly.

"No," I replied instantly.

"Definitely not," Travis affirmed, nodding in support.

"Okay then," the rabbi nodded, "Again, just asking. Then, let's talk about what you need to study before you convert."

"Our Hebrew sucks," Travis admitted, "and we could always use more Torah study."

The rabbi agreed to a loose plan, and we worked up an informal study schedule. There was no official reading list, but we could borrow books from the synagogue library whenever we wanted. There was no longer a syllabus, but the Jewish calendar provided us with a natural path forward when it came to studying holidays and Torah portions. We had no guest speakers in Rabbi Rubenstein's office, but I was welcome to pepper my fellow congregants with questions at every opportunity. As much as I loved my conversion classmates in Chicago, shifting gears to one-on-one study had benefits.

All of our subsequent meetings with the rabbi were quiet and relaxed. We were able to ask questions about the finer details of Jewish holidays and belief in order to make sure that we were prepared to commit to a lifetime of following those teachings. The rabbi called us on the phone once or twice a week while we read to him slowly and inaccurately from a Hebrew workbook. He admitted that he rarely tutored Hebrew anymore, so the fact that he made time to do so for us motivated me to try harder.

"That doesn't sound right," he would say when we butchered a word, "Try again."

Travis and I would look at each other and slowly sound out each word anew until we had the pronunciation right. Rabbi Rubenstein encouraged us to use the Hebrew version for things like *havdallah*, the ritual and prayers marking the end of the Sabbath. His encouragement pushed us to keep grappling with Hebrew when we were ready to scrap it.

When we had spare time, we read from our English translations of the Tanakh, starting with Genesis and working our way forward. The Jewish commentary on the early books of the Bible bears little resemblance to the Christian commentary. It was more or less the same story, but interpreted so differently that I hardly felt like I knew the stories at all. I pored over Jewish commentaries online in order to reframe my understanding. I often found myself nodding along in agreement, relieved and elated to find such sensible and practical teachings where I had once seen total malarkey.

"Did you know that some Jewish scholars say that the entire point of Genesis is only to show that the universe and humankind was designed with great intention?" I asked Travis one day, taking notes furiously on a legal pad. "A lot of Jews aren't wholly concerned with finding the remains of Noah's ark or proving that the universe could have been created in seven days."

Travis immersed himself in his own copy of the Tanakh, making similar comments to me about what he was learning from time to time. The more I read Torah commentaries online, the more I came to realize that the "point" of Jewish teachings were often deceptively simple.

The first time that we attended services, the rabbi paraded us around and introduced us to the other congregation members. We were overwhelmed but grateful for everyone's warmth. We tried *cholent* for the first time, and we found that we could actually follow along with services on Saturday mornings. We were accepted as if we'd always been Jewish. As my pregnancy dragged on and my belly grew, we made friends and attended holiday celebrations like any other synagogue member. When we showed up to the Shavuot study session or to Saturday *kiddush*, no one paid any attention to the fact that we happened to be converts. In fact, I'm sure there were people who didn't know we were converting at all. I stopped feeling like a student of Judaism and started feeling like a full-fledged Jew.

We had celebrated Hanukkah, Tu B'Shevat, Purim, and Passover in Chicago. This meant that we would celebrate Shavuot, Tisha B'Av, Rosh Hashanah, Yom Kippur, Sukkot, and Simchat Torah at our new synagogue in Michigan.

Shavuot is historically a harvest festival but now is used to celebrate the giving of the Torah at Mount Sinai. It comes after Passover in the spring but before

SHANNON GONYOU

the heavy heat of summer. On Shavuot, Jews read the
Ten Commandments, and there is usually all-night study
session to represent "being alert" and ready for the Torah.
If this sounds terribly taxing, don't worry, there are
usually several different flavors of cheesecake and other
dairy-based snacks to keep you going. (There are a lot of
explanations for why Shavuot involves consuming various
dairy products, but I long ago gave up on getting a final
answer). Study sessions cover any number of Jewish topics.
In this case, there were presentations on human trafficking,
honoring the Sabbath, and the Jewish concept of angels.
I was so tired from my unrelenting pregnancy insomnia
that I made Travis drive us home before midnight and was
fast asleep in the car while our fellow Jews studied on—
slightly anticlimactic but a good representation of the role
of study in Jewish life. In subsequent years, we took our
daughter to children's Shavuot events, which generally
involve too much ice cream and a story about how God
choose to give the Torah on humble Mt. Sinai, a lesson
about humility and the way that God can transform
something from mundane to spectacular.

Tisha B'Av takes place mid-summer. It remembers the
destruction of the First and Second Temples in Jerusalem,
so observant Jews spend the day fasting and sitting on
the ground to pray. Many Jews refer to Tisha B'Av as the
"rock bottom" of the Jewish calendar. It commemorates
a negative historical event, inviting us to reflect on our
own rock bottoms, failures, and fears. After Tisha B'Av,
we begin our long journey to the Jewish new year and
day of atonement, which take place as summer turns to
fall. Pregnant women don't usually fast, and if I sat on the

237

ground to pray, I would never be able to get back up. I skipped my first Tisha B'Av service and read some articles about the history of the temple and about the concept of "baseless hatred" instead.

Since Rosh Hashanah and Yom Kippur, referred to as the High Holidays, are the apex of the Hebrew calendar, our rabbi agreed that we should complete our conversion beforehand and celebrate the Jewish New Year as full-fledged Jews. By the time that early August came around, it was clear that our conversion was moving from the learning phase to the preparing-to-finalize-things phase. My nerves were all but gone at this point. I felt so much like I belonged that I needed it to be official.

CHAPTER 16

"You will find that it is necessary to let things go;
simply for the reason that they are heavy."
–C. JoyBell

I often thought back to the chaos of my Boston Synagogue experience while sitting through the more orderly Saturday morning service at my new *shul*. Everyone in Rabbi Rubenstein's congregation took services seriously enough, but 2 1/2 hours is a long time to focus. Pregnant women get hungry. Travis knew that I felt right at home when I snuck out a bag of carrots—my constant pregnancy craving—during services one Saturday and started to loudly crunch while the rabbi was praying.

"Are you serious?" he asked, sitting up straight and paying attention like he always did.

"Yeah," I said through a mouth full of carrot, "I'm pregnant!"

"Take the carrots into the kitchen," he hissed, his cheeks turning red.

"The rabbi won't care," I insisted. But after a few more anxious looks from Travis, I relented and took my bag to the kitchen. There were other men and women standing around chatting outside of the sanctuary, a few children hiding among the coatracks. While my old Catholic Church might have called this type of congregating "disrespectful," it gives going to *shul* a much more communal feeling. It says, "We're all friends here; some of us come to pray, and others come to distract our friends from prayer."

Giving everyone I encountered a smile or nod, I made my way to the kitchen, where another pregnant congregant was sneaking a pre-*kiddush* bagel.

"This is amazing," I told her animatedly, holding up my bag of carrots and gesturing around, "I never even left Mass to go to the bathroom. No one wanders around. And here, people are sneaking away for whiskey shots or social time."

"People get hungry—or bored," she shrugged innocently.

"I love it here," I sighed, crunching into yet another baby carrot.

I did love it at services even if I didn't always stay in my seat. Sermons given by a rabbi are similar to sermons given in Christian churches: lessons about that week's reading and thoughts about how to take the lessons of the Bible into the modern world. Rabbi Rubenstein was an excellent speaker—always calm, even-handed, and reflective. The rabbi's wife was hilarious, and when she graced us with her presence at Saturday services, we'd invariably end up laughing at something moderately inappropriate in the back of the sanctuary.

Once I even read a book during services, much to Travis's shock and horror. I wasn't disinterested in the service, but I had promised to return the book to the synagogue library that afternoon, and I had 30 very riveting pages to go. A tall gentleman seated near us leaned over and asked how the book was. In a soft voice, I carried on a brief conversation about the author's analysis of the Jewish concept of *tshuva* while prayers continued from the *bimah*. I felt like the old couple in the Boston Synagogue, chatting happily away in the middle of services. I felt like I belonged.

Even though our baby had yet to arrive, the rabbi pulled me aside one Saturday during *kiddush* and asked if Travis and I would be interested in joining a group of young parents.

"Did someone invite me?!" I asked, excited to be folded in to the social fabric of the *shul*.

"Yes, of course," the rabbi said with a confused smile. "Why wouldn't you be invited?"

"I don't know," I admitted, grabbing a handful of chocolate cookies and placing them on my paper plate. "I'm excited to be included. We would love to attend."

"Great," said the rabbi, "I'll let them know. Also, I saw the five cookies that you grabbed."

"Pregnant," I replied, shuffling away with my dessert held close.

Parents' group was great because there were two other pregnant women to commiserate with and a handful of toddlers to remind us that the arduous nine months were worth it. We gathered on Sunday mornings for bagels, eggs, and conversation. Making friends through a synagogue is not the same as making them through a church. It's not necessarily religion that unites us. We all attend the same synagogue, sure, but every family tends to have different religious practices from the family who sits next to them. Our conversations revolved around parenting, travel, recipes, and Costco discounts. Our meetings never turned into impromptu Bible studies or fiery religious debates. We mostly answered life's more mundane questions, such as how to operate a swim diaper and whether baked French toast is superior to the grilled variety.

"I'm excited to be a Jewish dad," Travis professed when we got back into our car after the first "play date."

"I'm excited to be a Jewish mom," I said wistfully, rubbing my stomach and wondering what my daughter would be like.

"You're already a Jewish mom," Travis said with an eye roll, "trying to force second helpings on people all the time."

"That is an unfair Jewish mother stereotype," I gasped in mock indignation.

"Is it?" he asked teasingly.

"Just drive," I replied, smacking him playfully on the shoulder.

When I was about eight months pregnant, I started experiencing bouts of false labor. I was slightly dilated, but this is not uncommon, even in a first pregnancy. Given our experience with pregnancy loss, I spent a lot of time anxiously counting the baby's kicks and fretting over her general well-being. I was cautious about every bite I ate and every cleaning product used on the surfaces of our home. I switched to walking and stretching in lieu of more vigorous exercise. Given the uncertainty surrounding our sweet girl's arrival, I asked Rabbi Rubenstein what would happen if she entered the world before my *beit din*.

"It's no big deal," he told me. "She can convert separately."

"You mean we have to dunk the baby in the water?" I asked skeptically.

"Not a newborn," he clarified. "But sure, they're fine. You take the baby into the *mikveh* when they're a little bigger and then they're Jewish, too."

I wasn't so sure about that plan. At home that night, we watched a YouTube video of the conversion of a cute, chubby baby boy. He, his mother, and the rabbi were all in the *mikveh* together (though the adults wore bathing suits for modesty).

"When I finish the blessing," the rabbi instructed, "let go of the child so that he can be immersed fully in the water. Once his head falls under the surface, we can pick him back up." The most important rule of the mikveh is that the water must touch every square centimeter of your skin. This means that adults take off all clothing, jewelry, lotion, and makeup before entering; babies and children must float in the water without being held or touched by their adult supervisor. The woman nodded nervously at the camera.

"We're ready," she told the rabbi uncertainly.

"I know," he said patiently. "Letting go is the hardest part." He said it wistfully in the way that rabbis often speak. I could tell that he wasn't talking about plunking the baby into the water but of how hard it is to let go of our parental fears in general. I took a deep breath and felt my shoulders relax.

By coincidence, we attended services in Ann Arbor that weekend, and the rabbi gave a sermon on parenting. He talked about the art of letting children be, and the Jewish idea that parenting is meant to raise independent adults rather than sheltered, dependent beings. Whether it was God or the community talking, I got the message. I needed to stop obsessing over every detail of the pregnancy. My daughter would arrive when she arrived, and there was little I could do to control the outcome.

As summer turned to fall, my daughter still securely in my belly, Rabbi Rubenstein talked to us about setting a date for the conversion. He expressed very timid reservations about whether we felt like we'd had enough time to study before making our conversion official.

"Studying is a lifelong process, Rabbi Rubenstein," I insisted, tossing out Jewish doctrine like a pro. "We're ready now. I want to go to the *mikveh* before the baby arrives, if possible."

Travis agreed that we already felt at home in Judaism and were eager to move forward. Being satisfied with our answers, the rabbi started assembling a *beit din*. They agreed to perform the conversion before the High Holidays so that we would be able to celebrate Rosh Hashanah and Yom Kippur as Jews. I was overjoyed.

The last thing that I had to do was write my conversion essay, which the rabbis overseeing my conversion would use to get to know me before the big day. Before the *beit din*, I sent all three participating rabbis an essay on why I had chosen my Hebrew name. Technically, the prompt had been to talk about why I wanted to be Jewish, but following the rules was never my thing.

I had chosen to be called Chava, the Hebrew name for Eve. Chava is also a character in *Fiddler on the Roof* who was Jewish and married a Christian man, so the irony wasn't totally lost on me. My affinity for Eve, who is often seen as a sort of enemy in Christianity, began with a study piece on Exodus 6:2–9:3 written by Rabbi Jack Moline of the Jewish Theological Seminary. This passage in Exodus recounts that the Israelites cried out to God over the conditions of their enslavement in Egypt, and God responds to their plea by liberating them. This story is simple enough. The Israelites were oppressed, so they cry out to their God, and God intervenes. But Moline asks a more complicated question about what would have been better: being enslaved and then freed by God, or never being enslaved to begin with?

Besides the fact that only the former makes a good story to pass down, Moline suggests that the answer to this question harkens back to Genesis. Before converting, I understood the story of Adam and Eve like this: naughty Eve was tempted by the evil serpent to eat the forbidden fruit, thus bringing disobedience and sin into the world. Mind you, evil must have predated the apple eating, or else the tree wouldn't know about it, either. Either way, it's implied that Eve made a crappy choice: what good is knowledge of good versus evil compared to the glory of living in Eden? In her greedy thirst for knowledge, Eve ruined our shot at living forever in paradise. She sinned, and we would therefore be generations of sinners. Putting aside for a moment that the Jewish concept of sin bears little resemblance to its Christian counterpart, this story has some gaps.

Moline asked a question that I had never had occasion to consider: what did God create the forbidden tree for in the first instance? Unless God likes snacking on knowledge apples, it had to have served a purpose. Christians may tend to see it as a test, but Moline says this: "To be liberated from their comprehensive dependence on God, they had to recognize the oppressiveness of surrendering their autonomy, even in paradise." At first blush, this notion is pretty radical. Did a Conservative rabbi actually suggest that a life in paradise with God could be oppressive? Yes, and maybe that shouldn't be so surprising. Modern-day Jews love to study more than any other group of people I know—we embrace knowledge rather than reject it as contrary to living a life of faith. Without knowledge, what would Eden really look like? Here we have the tradeoff: Adam and Eve could have lived out their days in "paradise," fully dependent on an all-knowing, all-demanding, obey-me-or-else kind of deity and been none the wiser. Given this, perhaps Eve knew something that the rest of us cannot see when we read the story of our supposed fall from grace: that in order to have a just, non-oppressive relationship with the divine and with one another, our eyes must be open.

It is better to be uncomfortable and aware rather than ignorant and in bliss. With knowledge, we can question whether the things around us are good or evil. We can even question the very God we worship. We see the brokenness, and we repair it. I think Eve is smarter than we gave her credit for. Like so many Jews before me, I wasn't going to accept faith without a little fight. I was, like Eve, bound to be a bit of a rebel. I was a natural-born apple biter. If the Conservative Judaism movement would take me anyway, I wanted in.

With my essay signed, sealed, and delivered, all there was to do was wait. A *beit din* is a private affair, so there were no YouTube videos to refer to this time. I resisted the urge to look up sample questions online. I had been promised by both Cantor Berke and Rabbi Rubenstein that the goal of a *beit din* is not to grill potential converts on the intricacies of Jewish law but to have a two-way conversation about the convert's interest in joining the Jewish community. On the day of our conversion, Travis and I packed up a couple of towels and made the hour-long drive from Ann Arbor to West Bloomfield. We didn't speak much.

When we arrived, Travis had to be taken back for the *hatafat dam* brit. Even though he was already circumcised,

Jewish law requires there to be a ritual pinprick in order to represent a convert becoming part of the covenant. This pinprick caused Travis anxiety since Liz first mentioned it. There had been so much buildup that I was nervous for him, too. Fortunately, he came back looking decidedly untraumatized.

"You okay?" I asked.

"Barely felt it," he admitted with obvious relief.

"Who's coming back to the *beit din* first?" Rabbi Rubenstein inquired.

"Let him go," I said, gesturing to Travis. He'd had his penis stabbed, after all, so I thought he deserved to get the *beit din* over with first. The rabbi led him to a back room while I remained in the lobby, snacking nervously on chocolate-covered raisins. My daughter kicked and rolled inside of me.

"This is it, pumpkin," I whispered to her softly, "You and Momma are both going to be Jewish this morning." She kicked me again, hard. I took this as a sign of approval. I was alone in the lobby now, left to stew in silence. I leaned against the window and felt the midday August sun warm my back. I gently kicked my sandal-clad foot back and forth. What a bizarre moment. Here I was, a non-Jew, about to make my case for conversion. Before noon, I would be Jewish. I would have, ostensibly, a whole new Jewish soul. I wondered if I would feel any different. I breathed in and out and tried to imagine what they were asking Travis. Always poetic and well-spoken, I was sure that he was going to give spectacular answers despite his initial misgivings about conversion.

It felt like he was gone for a century, but it was only 20 minutes. He emerged with a small smile, so I knew it wasn't too taxing. Now, I was up. I had always pictured a *beit din* being set up a bit like a court, with the three rabbis on a bench above me, looking down judgmentally. In reality, we were sitting in a conference room, all three rabbis on the same side of the table, twisting in their swivel chairs and waiting patiently for my arrival. One was staring longingly out the window, and the other was leaned back casually.

"Why don't you start by telling us what initially made you want to become Jewish?" Rabbi Rubenstein suggested. The question was meant to be a softball to ease me in but was somehow hard to answer despite how many times I had practiced my response.

"I've tried to explain it to so many people in the past couple of years." I told them. "The answer evades me. Ever since I encountered Judaism, I have been enamored. There are so many ways to be a Jew, and yet the community remains cohesive despite the diversity of belief. I have always loved that Judaism is history, culture, food, language, and lifelong study. It's so much more than reading and believing in the Torah. In fact, many Jews don't believe in the Torah in a literal way, and some haven't read it since childhood. Judaism is a world unto itself, and I've known for a long time that I belong in it. I was hopelessly envious of my Jewish classmates."

"Why?" asked one of the rabbis in surprise. "Why would you feel jealous?"

"Because they had Judaism, and I didn't," I explained, "And I felt like I could never have it. I didn't think conversion was practical. When I started practicing, like when I lit Hanukkah candles for the first time, I felt like a fraud. But I've come to realize, obviously, that Judaism can belong to anyone who is sincerely drawn to it. I don't feel like a fraud anymore, and I don't have to envy my friends who grew up Jewish. I'm joining the tribe later in life, but from my perspective, I'm joining right on time."

There were nods of approval. I relaxed. This wasn't so bad.

"What are you more drawn to," a different rabbi asked, "the ritual aspects of Judaism, or the community aspects?"

"When it comes to our family," I answered, "both will be equally important. I can't wait for my daughter to attend Hebrew school and Jewish summer camp. I am excited about a lifetime of celebrating Jewish holidays and lifecycle events with my people, but I'm also grateful that Judaism helps us sanctify the smaller moments in life: blessings before meals, candles on Shabbat, and thinking about what to cook and how to dress. Judaism gives you a hundred chances to make each moment special, even holy. I'm excited for that, too."

The rabbi nodded in response. My answer was duly accepted.

"Why didn't you convert when you were in college?" another rabbi asked.

"I don't know," I answered honestly. "Like I said, mostly fear of rejection. Also, fear of change. Fear of judgment. And the fact that I was both busy and low-key starving myself. Of course, I'm busy now, but Judaism refused to go away, and it was time that I make time for it. This is my home."

They asked questions, and I answered them. They also responded to my answers and turned the interview into more of a discussion. Twenty minutes flew by.

I went back into the lobby to wait with Travis for their verdict. It took less than five minutes for them to emerge, Rabbi Rubenstein smiling widely.

"Ready to dunk?" he asked.

We were ready.

CHAPTER 17

"Beloved are proselytes by God, for the Bible
everywhere uses the same epithet of them as of
Israel." — *Talmud, Gerim 4:3*

Immersing yourself in the *mikveh* has to be the closest feeling we can get to being enveloped in the warmth and silence of the womb. When I waded carefully down the marble steps of the *mikveh*, I was startled by the warmth of the water. It was warmer than bathwater, and totally still except for the ripples that my moving legs created. A *mikveh* is basically a fancy, large bathroom. There is a shower area where you can undress and rinse, and of course the *mikveh* itself, a deep rectangle full of clear, warm water. The rabbis were waiting on the other side of the wooden door that led to the hallway. A female attendant had been sent in to observe my immersion. She stood at the top of the stairs, clutching a towel so that she could hand it to me when I was finished.

When the rabbis indicated that they were ready, I descended the rest of the steps and stood in the center of the deep part of the *mikveh*. The warm water came up to my chest. I stood on my toes to give myself some space. The *mikveh* blessing was inscribed in beautiful blue letters on the wall in front of me.

"I'm going to recite the blessing," I called to the rabbis outside. My voice echoed loudly off of the walls of the chamber.

"Okay, we're ready," Rabbi Rubenstein called back from the other side of the wooden door.

One dunk, the blessings, two more dunks. That was all. Then I'd be Jewish. Going to the *mikveh* felt like a monumental occasion. I wanted to take my time. I took in my surroundings. I enjoyed the silence in the room, my breathing, and the *mikveh* attendant shifting from foot to foot above me.

At the time of conversion, I recited two blessings: the blessing acknowledging God's commandment to use the *mikveh* and the *shehecheyanu*, a blessing recited on special occasions. Some converts also recite the *Shema* in order to profess belief in the oneness of God, a core Jewish belief. I say the *Shema* every week in services now, but it wasn't one of the *mikveh* blessings that my rabbi uses.

With a deep, calm breath, I fell backwards into the water for the first time. When I was fully submerged, I let my arms float alongside me and my hair swirl around my face. It's wasn't like being underwater in a swimming pool. The water of the *mikveh* was hot on the sensitive skin of my face, but not uncomfortable. Because the *mikveh* is such a small, enclosed space, no sound at all pervades the stillness of your underwater world. As I floated momentarily beneath the surface of the water, I felt exactly like my daughter must have felt at that moment—safely enveloped in the private world of the womb. It was peaceful. I came back up to the surface with a gasp and pushed my wet hair out of my eyes. I didn't need to read the blessing from the wall. I had memorized it and practiced it plenty of times. I recited it from memory in gorgeous Hebrew, after which I recited the *shehecheyanu* loud and clear. It was like I was shouting my words up to the heavens, lest God be unaware that there was a conversion scheduled for today. I think my volume surprised even the rabbis.

"Wow. Amen," one of the rabbis said with admiration in his voice.

I dunked myself under the water twice more, savoring the feeling of floating weightlessly beneath the surface each time. When I stood up, I looked at the *mikveh* attendant for approval.

"*Mazal tov!*" she squeaked, holding out the towel for me as I walked back up the steps and out of the warm water. I wrapped the towel around my shoulders and looked at myself in the mirror. I was wet and happy and very Jewish. My daughter gave another kick of approval.

The celebration of conversion was very subdued. The rabbis offered an enthusiastic "*Mazal tov!*" and presented us with signed certificates. After that, we both returned to work for the day. I had marked the time off in my work calendar as "busy" but in retrospect it would have been significantly more comical to jot down "becoming a Jew." Alas.

In the evening, we cut a kosher chocolate-raspberry cake and enjoyed it in our dining room alone. I didn't think my parents would be excited enough to warrant inviting them over for dessert. Travis's parents are always happy to celebrate anything with us, but we hadn't been very vocal about our conversion. We were sure of ourselves and very proud to be Jewish, but we had found that religious conversion, especially to Judaism, turned out to be a bit of an awkward topic of conversation among Christian friends and family. As I enjoyed my cake, I texted my close Jewish friends to let them know that I was in. I appreciated their well wishes very much.

Because the *mikveh* is a private affair, new Jews are usually introduced to their congregation on the Saturday following the conversion. It's not a big party like a teenage Bar or Bat Mitzvah, but it was nice. On the appointed day, we were called up to the *bimah* to bless the Torah. We practiced the blessing for hours ahead of time and absolutely nailed it.

"They started learning Hebrew a few months ago," the rabbi mentioned proudly to the congregation after we had finished.

He then read our Hebrew names and said a long prayer for each of us. Travis and I, in turn, recited something like a statement of faith and made promises to the Jewish community, primarily that we would stick with them forever and cherish the traditions that we had adopted. I meant every word.

As we made our way back to our seats, navigating hugs and handshakes along the way, the rabbi emphasized that the congregation was not to speak of our conversion again. This is an important part of Jewish law: that converts not be constantly reminded of their status. I was happy about the conversion, but I was glad that the rabbi was giving us a break from opining on it for a little while. It was nice to sit back down in our usual seats in the back row being *halachically* Jewish, full stop.

Now, of course, people ask me about my conversion all the time. Not usually on purpose. When they ask what my parents are doing for Passover, I usually have to remark that my parents are not Jewish. When people ask why a Jewish girl has such a non-Jewish name, I reveal that I converted. My conversion comes up in conversations about Ashkenazi cooking and Jewish summer camp. It comes up when I butcher Hebrew or admit that I still don't know how to build a *sukkah*. It comes up when it does, and I don't make a fuss about it. Even if my soul was always Jewish, I think that choosing a Jewish life is something to be proud of.

While services were still in full swing, someone came to grab Travis and I to congratulate us on our conversion.

"Come with me," he said, "It's time for *Kiddush* Club."

"Time for what?" I asked.

"Just come," he beckoned. We followed him and a large group of others out of the sanctuary even as someone was still up at the *bimah* chanting. He took us to a small room in the back of the synagogue. It was the size of a large closet and lined with mirrors, with a lone cabinet in the back of the room. My friend Monica flung open the cabinet to reveal at least 15 different bottles of liquor.

"*Kiddush* Club!" an older Russian man exclaimed, "We all take a shot of whiskey because this is the part of services that get really boring."

I burst into laughter. This was so very Jewish.

"I can't drink," I pointed out, poking at my still-pregnant belly, "but how about a celebratory orange juice shot?" The group obliged, setting me up with a small cup of juice and two Oreos. Someone gave a toast to the new converts. Everyone shouted "*Mazal tov*," and we all drank. There were a few minutes of socializing, and then we all filtered back into the sanctuary as if we hadn't thrown a mini-party in the middle of a religious service.

This was amazing. I was home.

After we were officially introduced as Jews, it was time to turn to High Holiday preparation. The High Holidays include Rosh Hashanah (New Year on the Hebrew calendar) and Yom Kippur (the Day of Atonement). These holidays tend to be the only ones that non-Jews are familiar with outside of Hanukkah and Passover, though that doesn't stop people from forgetting when they take place. Because they aren't federal holidays, I let my colleagues know that I'd be using a few vacation days.

One does not simply arrive at the High Holidays without preparation. A menu has to be planned for both holidays, family gatherings negotiated (more complicated for families who actually celebrate, unlike the families of converts), and Yom Kippur involves significant spiritual reflection. Before Yom Kippur, we are supposed to apologize to those we've hurt and take steps to rectify the harms. I made a to-do list and got to work.

First up was the synagogue's Rosh Hashanah apple-picking event. Apples are one of the predominant foods of the holiday because they symbolize sweetness and their round shape alludes to the cycle of the year. They're healthier than Christmas cookies, anyway. When we went to the community's Rosh Hashanah apple-picking event at a local orchard, the rabbi took care to introduce us to everyone. We felt like mini-celebrities. Storing two cinnamon-sugar donuts for safekeeping, I shook hands with Jews from Ann Arbor and all of the Detroit suburbs. A new Jew entering a community—whether they converted or recently moved into town—is a happy event. Everyone was thrilled to meet us and even more excited that we were recent converts. Over the centuries, Jewish communities have experienced immeasurable losses. Adding back to the community through conversion is usually treated like cause for joy and celebration. The warmth with which we were received was touching.

"Do you have any questions about labor?" one of my new acquaintances asked me with concern. "I'm a labor anesthesiologist. Let me know if I can help with anything."

"I think I'm all set," I said, "But really, thank you."

"Remind me of your due date?" asked a friendly woman in his friend group. "I might be on call around then." She was an obstetrician. Apparently, medicine is a very popular profession in the Jewish community.

"Are you moving to Ann Arbor?" another woman asked. "I can give you advice about neighborhoods."

"Yeah, I can tell you all about the daycares in the area," someone else chimed in. Throughout the morning, other

Jews chimed in with recipes for slow-cooker applesauce, brisket, and other Rosh Hashanah meal ideas.

"I know you don't have a family cookbook," an older woman told me, "I'm happy to pass along any recipes you might need. I have the perfect recipe for vegan mac and cheese that you can serve with a meat-based meal!"

Overwhelmed but grateful, I shoved more apples into my bag and nodded.

"Thanks so much," I told her. We exchanged business cards and email addresses with a handful of people as we enjoyed the beautiful fall weather and loaded up on different varieties of apples. I was grateful that all of these people who had never met me were eager to do anything they could to ease our anxiety about childbirth, Jewish holidays, and beyond. We went home with two pounds of apples with which to make our Rosh Hashanah treats and also a handful of new friends. Jewish camaraderie is not conditional on believing the same things as the rest of the congregation; that feels special. No one wanted to save my soul or anything like that. They truly just wanted to welcome me and share a recipe, no strings attached.

It would have been wise to actually use their recipes for our first Rosh Hashanah. We invited our parents over for dinner even though they didn't really know what was going on, and I took a chance on some un-tested online recipes. I made a vegetarian jackfruit brisket with roasted carrots and an apple pound cake. Although I botched the jackfruit brisket and the cake was on the bland side, everyone pretended that the meal was amazing, which

I appreciated. My mom looked unsure about my soupy, subpar brisket, but she said nothing.

"Now," Travis explained with a grin, "we dip our apples in honey to symbolize having a sweet new year."

"*Shana Tova!*" my mother-in-law chirped happily, proud that she had looked up the Hebrew well-wishes ahead of time.

"*Shana Tova,*" I nodded to her with a smile. It was going to be a sweet year. We were finally Jewish, and our daughter was still secure inside my womb. Our families were warming up, however slowly, to the fact that we were Jewish.

On the heels of Rosh Hashanah comes Yom Kippur. I gently reminded my colleagues that I would be out for another holiday and started to make plans for how I would eat and drink during services. Yom Kippur is a fasting holiday, and Jewish fasting is quite different from Catholic fasting, which allows for the consumption of water or even juice. Pregnant women mostly skip the fasts, so I set out to make plans for stealthily consuming water and snacks to keep myself going during the morning-to-night services. It is quite literally an all-day affair.

We had planned to drive back to Chicago to celebrate Yom Kippur with our old community at Mishkan, but I was in a losing battle with pregnancy insomnia and wound up fainting less than 48 hours before we were supposed to leave town. We decided to play it safe and attend services at our congregation in Michigan instead.

When the rabbi noticed that we were unexpectedly in attendance, Travis was invited to participate in opening the ark where the Torah is stored. Being invited to participate in services is always an honor but especially on an important holiday.

"I don't know what I'm supposed to do," Travis hissed at me nervously.

"Copy everyone else," I suggested, wrapping my prayer shawl protectively around my shoulders and belly.

"Why don't you come up, too?" he asked.

"I can't stand for that long," I argued, "My feet are already swollen from the *Amidah*." (The *Amidah* is a long prayer during which you stand if you're able).

Travis did a fine job on his own.

After a long day of prayers, services concluded with one of the congregation members taking out his guitar for *Havdallah*, a ceremony that translates to "separation." Flames were kindled in the dark sanctuary, and everyone looped their arms around one another and swayed to the melody. It was beautiful.

After services, the daughter of the synagogue's president invited us to their home to break the fast. Both of us were pregnant so there was no fast to break, but I wasn't going to turn down the opportunity.

"We're invited to their break-fast?" Travis asked when I passed along the invitation, "They're, like, synagogue royalty!"

"Don't be weird," I told him sternly. "Let's go eat, and then I'm going to bed."

That night, belly full of soup and bread, I slept more soundly than I had in weeks. Now that I'd experienced the High Holidays as a Jew, my sense of belonging had sunk in.

The fall holidays on the Hebrew calendar are unrelenting, but in a good way. Before the baby's due date, we still had Sukkot and Simchat Torah. I was growing very large and uncomfortable, so I let Travis take the lead on celebrating those holidays on behalf of both of us.

"There were so many instructions for building the *sukkah*," Travis explained when he came home from helping the men's club construct one at our synagogue. A *sukkah* is basically a dining tent covered with tree branches; we eat meals in it during the fall. It's similar to what one would expect of a harvest festival, though when it comes to Judaism, there are always several layers of symbolism and theology. Our rabbi talked us through most of them, but mostly I was glad that we would have an incentive to spend more time on our deck before the weather turned cold. I suppose you could compare *Sukkot* to Thanksgiving—it's a time to enjoy crisp weather, meals with friends, and share a sense of gratitude for our food.

"The frustrations of building the perfect *sukkah* sound very Jewish," I agreed. "Was it hard?"

"Not really," he said, "I mean, the *sukkah* is built the same way every year, but no one writes down proper instructions, so somehow it still took us the better part of three hours. I was starting to sweat."

"*Kol hakavod*," I smirked, which essentially means "well done" in Hebrew.

Simchat Torah is another fall holiday that celebrates having read the entire Torah over the course of the year. On Simchat Torah, we unwind the Torah scroll and begin reading anew at Genesis, symbolizing the fact that Jewish study has no end point. Typically, the holiday involves a lot of standing, dancing, and parading. None of those things sounded appealing to me in my very pregnant condition. I ended up staying home to work, for which my colleagues must have been thankful.

"I think my colleagues are sick of me taking vacation days," I admitted to Travis while firing off emails on Simchat Torah.

"They should be thankful that their holidays are generally protected by federal law," he replied unsympathetically.

"Touché. Do you think any of my colleagues remember that I wasn't Jewish last year or the year before?"

"Not a chance at your firm," he snickered. It was true: the last thing my firm was apt to do was pay attention to our personal lives.

"Fair enough," I agreed. "It's kind of a relief, honestly."

Travis and I continued going to services on Saturdays. Since our synagogue was 45 minutes from our home (and our hospital), I started packing a hospital bag in case my water decided to break in the presence of God. The wait was getting harder and harder. The older women at *shul* would stare at my belly and make predictions about my due date, while the other men gave Travis detailed instructions on how to drive to the hospital during labor and what to pack for the journey. We were all ready. Jewish and ready.

CHAPTER 18

"I believe the choice to become a mother is the choice to become one of the greatest spiritual teachers there is." –*Oprah Winfrey*

On the day I went to the *mikveh*, my Jewish self was born. I emerged from the womb of the *mikveh* a Jew. Shortly after, my daughter emerged from my womb a Jew, as well. In the end, she was only seven days early. Labor was long and arduous, and my daughter came out with the umbilical cord wrapped tightly around her neck. By some miracle, I was too exhausted to be scared. I knew she would be okay.

"What's her name?" the resident and attending physician asked mid-labor. I was feeling very relaxed thanks to my epidural.

"Ora. It means light. It's appropriate because she's right on time for Hanukkah," I smiled. Ora is our daughter's Hebrew name; she has a different English name that's listed on her birth certificate and that we use on a daily basis at home.

"Right," Dr. Baruch, the Jewish attending physician, agreed. "Except, with Hanukkah, the oil lasted longer than expected. Your pregnancy was shorter than expected. A different kind of miracle!"

"I don't get all of the Jewish inside jokes," the resident admitted, "but it's a lovely name."

With my brown hair and dark eyes, I can pass as an American-Ashkenazi Jew. My daughter came into the world with messy red hair and sapphire blue eyes. I could already anticipate a chorus of people telling me that "she doesn't look very Jewish." I loved her immediately, and she is very much Jewish.

The attending physician offered us a hearty *"Mazal tov!"* My husband shook his hand and thanked him. Although there are less than six million Jews in America, I have found that one is always there when you need them most. As Travis thanked Dr. Baruch for his help, I drifted off to sleep.

When my daughter had been bathed and nursed, I put her in a tiny newborn onesie. It was white with black font that said, "Chai, I'm new here." Chai is the Hebrew word for life, so it was a sweet play on words.

"What does that onesie say?" a nurse asked, squinting at the Hebrew letter on my daughter's bitty newborn chest.

"Oh, it's a Jewish thing," I said shyly. She shrugged and went back to her paperwork.

We kept the parade of visitors small. Only my mom and my in-laws came to meet the baby. It was already flu season, and we were cautious to the point of paranoia.

"Your grandmother would be obsessed with this baby," my mother gushed as she looked into my daughter's bright blue eyes.

"I know," I agreed, "I wish she was alive to meet her." I considered it a good sign that my grandmother's name, Ora, happened to be a fairly common Hebrew name. Everything felt like it was meant to be.

The newborn days with my daughter were a blur. We spent most of our day trying to get her to latch and cleaning up various messes that she had created. People brought us food, which we gratefully heated up whenever the baby was taking a snooze. Our Jewish friends sent us gifts for the baby: a colorful *hanukkiah*, a nightlight featuring a six-pointed star, piles of blankets. Since our Judaica collection was still very small, we cherished all of the new additions.

We spent three weeks in our house with the baby before we started feeling a bit antsy. Our parents visited in the evenings, but we desperately longed to introduce our community to the baby. On the third Shabbat after her arrival, we bundled her up and took her to our synagogue. We were grinning from ear to ear when we marched through the *shul* doors with our new addition in tow at last.

"Wow," the rabbi breathed as he stood over her car seat in amazement.

"THAT is a beautiful baby!" an older woman declared.

"We need more red-headed Jews," someone else agreed, offering me a thumb's up as if I had planned the hair color myself.

"*Mazal tov*," everyone echoed, admiring our daughter's fuzzy red hair from a respectful distance.

Travis beamed with pride. With my daughter secured tightly to his chest in a baby carrier, Travis wrapped himself in a prayer shawl and swayed to the rhythm of Saturday prayers. Ora slept like an angel for the entire service, hiding her little face under Travis' *tallit*.

"Let me see these tiny pants," my friend Monica gushed, holding up my daughter's spare outfit. "I miss these tiny clothes so much."

"It's going to fly by," the synagogue president told me.

"That's what they say," I sighed, running my finger over my daughter's little forehead.

Ora woke up with a vengeance once services were over. I breastfed her in the back of the sanctuary while everyone else was enjoying *kiddush*. I think it was the first time that I went to services and left without touching the dessert table.

Three weeks after Ora's first trip to services, we returned to the synagogue for her naming ceremony. I tell Christians that it's like a baptism with no water. That doesn't really capture the nature of a baby naming, but sometimes a simple explanation works best. Her naming ceremony was quite similar to the one that the rabbi performed for us after our conversion but with less participation on my child's part. For most of the service, I held the baby against my chest while her blue eyes darted around suspiciously. This time, in a sleep-deprived haze, we completely butchered the blessings in front of our entire family.

My daughter was soundly asleep when her Jewish name was called out to the congregation. We placed her hands on the Torah to symbolize handing over to her the history and tradition of the Jewish people. How easy it had been for her to take her space in the stream of Jewish history. No classes, no awkward trips to the Kosher grocery store to decipher what it means for pretzels to be "*pareve*." She was Jewish from the day that she was born. I was proud to have given her that gift. Once again, the people around us shouted "*Mazal tov*" and accepted our daughter into their sacred space. My mother smiled stiffly but seemingly concluded that the whole Jewish ordeal wasn't so bad, after all. It was her first time in a synagogue, and her first time meeting our rabbi. When I asked her how she liked it, she assured me that the latkes at *Kiddush* were very good.

That evening, Travis lit our *Havdallah* candle, held on to my daughter, half asleep in her orange pumpkin pajamas, and sang the blessings for the end of the Sabbath. I snuck a video of him rocking her and singing in front of the candle. I sent it to our rabbi in the morning.

"This is beautiful," he texted back.

"He actually cried when he saw that video," his wife texted me later.

Days after the baby naming, my post-labor bleeding finally stopped. I had not been to the *mikveh* since my conversion, and I told Travis I might like to go again.

"Are you going to go every time you get your period?" he asked curiously. We had never discussed it before. Observant women, or at least those who observe the laws of *niddah*, visit the *mikveh* after their menstrual cycle ends each month. The tradition is ancient and somewhat divisive in modern Jewish life. Our conversion class had read and discussed an article about whether the *mikveh* should be "reclaimed" for non-traditional purposes. Some women feel that *niddah* treats menstruation as something dirty and feel insulted by it. Others feel that *mikveh* observance is overly gendered. However, I also read articles stressing that the ritual impurity discussed in Leviticus has nothing to do with moral purity. A Chabad website states that, "Impurity is neither evil nor dangerous and it is not something tangible. Impurity is a spiritual state of being, the absence of purity, much as darkness is the absence of light." It further emphasizes that the concept of purity and impurity in the Torah is unique to Jewish life and has no parallel in the modern age.

To be fair, the *mikveh* is used for a lot of purposes in Jewish life outside of conversion and menstruation, but I didn't know many other Jews who made a monthly visit. For some reason, I felt called to keep going. The *mikveh* seemed, to me, like a physical and spiritual spa trip. Being submerged in the *mikveh* is like being in another world. Time seems to stop when the warm water presses in on you. I couldn't deny that it felt powerful to me. It would also be one of the first hours that I spent away from my newborn if I went.

"I don't think I'm going to go every month," I admitted, "I can only take it one month at a time, and I really want to go."

Not everyone would approve of my going to the *mikveh* some months and not others, but welcome to being Jewish. Other peoples' practices don't have to concern me and vice versa. The *mikveh* where we had converted was too far away, so I emailed our local Chabad to make an appointment at their facility.

"Are they going to let you use it?" Travis asked.

"I think so," I told him. "My practice is different from theirs, but a Jew is a Jew."

"Okay," he said skeptically.

Chabad was only moderately skeptical about my appointment. I explained that I had recently had a baby and my bleeding was over.

"Have you been here before?" the *mikveh* lady asked.

"No, I moved here from Chicago," I told her. This was true. There was no point in bringing up my conversion at this juncture. I didn't want to go down that rabbit hole, and I shouldn't have to.

"I'm sorry to ask this," she said, "but are you Jewish?"

"Yes," I told her.

"Good," she sighed. "It's Ann Arbor. We get a lot of hippies hoping to have an experience."

"I'm Jewish," I assured her.

"Do you know the rules? Do you need me to go over anything? When did the bleeding stop?"

"Nine days ago," I told her.

"Do you want to come tonight? You shouldn't delay if it has been nine days."

"I'm free tonight," I said. I was free every night, given that I was on maternity leave. "Oh. Wait. No. I have fake nails on," I groaned. "I'll need time to remove them. How about tomorrow?" Nail polish and fake nails are prohibited in the *mikveh*. I had put them on days before and had totally forgotten. It was going to be painful to peel them off.

"That's fine," she said, "I'll arrange for someone to meet you there."

I spent all evening soaking off my fake nails, and the next evening I went to the *mikveh* after dark, freshly showered and shivering in the brutal December wind. Chabad only allows women to use the *mikveh* after sundown in order to preserve a woman's modesty. The woman who met me was slightly older than myself and dressed in the typical long black skirt and thick winter sweater. Out of respect, I had dressed modestly in a loose green sweater dress and black tights.

"What's your name?" the attendant asked as she let me inside.

"Shannon," I told her.

Her eyes narrowed suspiciously. "Chana?" she asked.

"Shannon," I repeated.

"Shayna?" she asked.

"Shannon, like the river in Ireland."

"Oh," she said.

"Call me Chava."

"Okay," she agreed. "You look way too alert to be freshly postpartum, Chava."

I took it as a compliment.

"My daughter sleeps through the night, other than nursing once or twice," I beamed.

"Don't tell people that," she chuckled, "they'll be jealous. I have seven kids, and none of them slept through the night before two months."

My head swam at the mention of seven kids, but I didn't show my surprise.

"I'll get undressed and get going," I told her, handing over my *mikveh* fee and taking off my glasses.

"Okay. Do you know what you're doing?"

"Yeah, yeah," I assured her, "I can get ready on my own." I'd only done it once before, but this convert knew the rules. I checked myself for stray bits of nail glue, loose hairs, dirt under the fingernails, food in the teeth. After I removed my jewelry, I headed out to the *mikveh* chamber.

"Do you dunk three or seven times?" my *mikveh* attendant asked.

"Three," I replied. I had forgotten that some Orthodox women dip seven times. Maybe I should have said seven.

I quite like the *mikveh*. But having committed to three, I waded in. "Your water is so hot!" I called in surprise.

"Too hot?" she asked, concern in her voice, "It hasn't been used this week. I can adjust it."

"No, it's okay," I promised, wading deeper and taking a breath. It didn't surprise me that Ann Arbor had a small number of *mikveh* users.

I was feeling a little self-conscious about my Judaism, so I made sure to pronounce the blessings very loudly and with flawless Hebrew. The attendant seemed confused by me, as if she thought something was off about my Jewishness. When I emerged from the *mikveh* and dressed, she seemingly gave up on trying to figure out what was wrong with me and asked if I'd like to come over for Shabbos dinner some time. I said yes.

When I disappeared back into the dark, snowy night, I felt refreshed. My hair was starting to freeze on the walk back to my parking spot, but something about immersing in the *mikveh* made me feel like a new woman. The days of pregnancy and the early postpartum days were done. There was only the rest of my life to look forward to.

I was lucky enough to have a long maternity leave. We passed most of our days nursing and watching the snow fall, braving a walk in the cold winter air once or twice a week when the baby would cooperate with getting into her tiny cardigan. Most of our friends worked during the week, so the stream of visitors was modest. At some point, one of my mom's oldest friends came to visit us and the baby, and she asked about why we had converted.

"You were SO Catholic before," she exclaimed, "I don't get it."

"We *looked* SO Catholic," I clarified. "I don't really do things halfway. That's not my personality. But I guess you never know what's going on in someone's life, you know? I don't feel like I have to go through the motions of Judaism. I don't have to pretend. I don't have to shove down my questions. Jewish is just who I am, and I'm really happy."

"Okay, I'm happy for you," she offered before letting her attention wander to Ora's perfect tiny feet. After that, none of our other visitors asked about the conversion. They might glance at the Judaica table or stumble when inquiring about our holiday plans, but everyone seemed to adopt a respectful silence about the situation.

When I was cleared to resume light exercise, I told Travis that I was going to join a local Fit4Mom class. The stroller-friendly class format would allow me to get out of the house without having to find a sitter for my daughter.

"The only weird thing is that the class near us meets at a mega church," I told Travis,

"I don't think that's weird," Travis said. "That church is huge."

"Do you think I'm allowed to go?" I asked hesitantly. "I think Jews frown upon wandering into Christian spaces."

"You're not wandering aimlessly," he laughed. "You're going to a fitness class. Jewish friends showed up to our Catholic wedding," he reminded me. "Just go."

That was all of the encouragement that I needed. As fate would have it, there were two other Jewish women at the class the first time I attended. The church in question owned a giant community center with a snack shop, two fireplaces, an indoor playscape, and a soccer field. I strained my ears to hear whether they were playing Christian rock music in the background, but it was a Disney soundtrack. I started going two or three times per week. I would work out with the other parents, purchase a blueberry muffin, and hang out to chat for an hour or two while older children ran around chasing soccer balls across the turf. It was really, really nice to have that community while Travis was at work.

"There is a New Testament quote in the nursing room," I reported back to Travis after the first class, "but otherwise they welcome all sorts of people—Jewish parents, Muslim parents, queer couples. I'm pleasantly surprised."

"That sounds like what Christianity was meant to be," Travis affirmed.

"Yeah," I agreed, "it is. But I'm glad we're Jewish."

"Me, too," he said.

Maternity leave passed much more quickly after I found the Fit4Mom classes. I blinked, and it was time for Purim. While we were adjusting to new parenthood, we hadn't really been able to enjoy the routines of Jewish life. We all slept through Hanukkah in the weeks after my daughter joined us, and we could never remember when Shabbat started and stopped. Days and nights pass in a sleepy blur with newborns. I wasn't ready to leave my daughter with a babysitter to go to a *megillah* reading (even after four months, I was not prepared to separate with her). Instead, I ordered her an adorable baby pineapple costume with a spiky hat, and we made plans to go to a local Purim carnival. I invited my mom to come with me.

"I don't really know what it *is*," my mom protested. I gave her a truncated version of the story of Purim.

"The Jews escaped mass murder once again, and we celebrate with carnivals and parties. The end!" I finished.

"I don't get why everyone wanted to kill the Jews," my mom sighed.

"Are you coming to the carnival or not?" I asked.

"We can go for a little while," my mom agreed, still looking a bit skeptical about the whole thing.

"That's all we need," I agreed. I put my tiny child into her pineapple costume and we drove across town to Temple Beth Emeth. The scene was similar to my old public-school fundraisers: there were children gleefully playing carnival games, a raffle, a cake-walk, and crafts. My mother relaxed. We blended right in and let my daughter observe the festivities, her little eyes darting around suspiciously. I suggested that we buy some food.

"I don't know what they have here!" my mom, ever the picky eater, hissed at me.

"I think they have pizza from a chain restaurant," I told her with an eye roll. "They're not going to make you eat gefilte fish."

"Oh," my mom said cautiously, "that's okay, then."

Purim, from my perspective, was a success. I got to introduce my infant daughter and my mother to the joy of one of my favorite holidays. It wasn't as raucous as our first Purim with Mishkan in Chicago, but it was perfect.

I pivoted from Purim right to planning a killer Passover menu. I had a large kitchen in Michigan and was no longer being assaulted by constant morning sickness. I started gathering ingredients with fervor.

Apparently, much like when the Jews fled Egypt, Passover would be a time of fleeing for our family, too. Travis had always worked for a firm in Detroit, and I had always worked for a firm in Chicago. Exactly a year after we had decided to move from Chicago to Michigan, it became clear that we'd need to move from Michigan back to Chicago. We had gotten comfortable with our lives in Michigan, but keeping both of us employed had turned into some sort of Olympic sport. There were more tears shed over the impending move, but we did what we had to do.

We said goodbye to our new Jewish friends in Michigan and apologized profusely to Rabbi Rubenstein for dropping in and out so quickly. We promised to maintain our synagogue membership from afar. I emailed Liz and let her know we'd be returning to Chicago. Rabbi Rubenstein was sad; Liz was elated.

"Can we revisit that award for most moves between Detroit and Chicago?" Travis groaned as we started to organize our belongings for packing.

"Sadly not," I told him. "But we're lucky to have such strong communities in both cities." And we were lucky. When we left Chicago for Michigan, it felt like we had come home—to the area where we had attended high school and college and where our parents lived and delighted in their new granddaughter. But when we moved from Michigan back to Chicago, that felt like going home, too. It was the city where we had made our own way as a married couple. The city where we discovered Judaism and conceived three children. It was sad to be away from Michigan, and it was good to be back in Chicago.

That summer in Chicago was long and hot. Without many Jewish holidays to focus on, we found ourselves going through the motions of a Jewish life without much thought. It turns out that my post-conversion life was a lot like my pre-conversion life. We worked, we fretted over our daughter's health, we took family trips to the Shedd Aquarium, and we spoiled the baby with croissants from French Quiche. The biggest difference was probably Friday night Shabbat observance, where we turned off our laptops and lit our candles. After a week of furious typing and answering emails while bouncing a baby, unplugging allowed us to take a deep breath. My daughter would always be the first to tear off a hunk of Travis's fresh-baked challah. When our candles burned down, we took long, slow walks around DePaul's campus, relishing a chance to focus on our surroundings instead of our vibrating phones. On Shabbat morning, we would bake cinnamon rolls (affectionately called "Shabbat cinnies" in our house) and video chat with grandparents. Both cooking and video chatting on Shabbat are technically prohibited, but they are a cherished part of our family Shabbat practice.

And so it went, a Jewish practice slowly building itself in our home. Candles on Friday, vegetarian food in the kitchen, a Hebrew lullaby here or there. Our daughter started crawling and using sign language to communicate with us. It was magical. By the time the High Holidays came back around, I was shocked that we had been Jews for a full year.

"It's our convertiversary!" I told Travis giddily.

We attended an outdoor *taschlich*. The exercise involves thinking about your wrongdoings and what you want to change in the next year, transferring your wrongdoings metaphorically onto bread or rocks or something similar, and then casting them away into the water. The sun was bright as we walked from our condo toward Lake Michigan. Our daughter bobbed along on Travis's shoulders as we enjoyed the fall breeze and reflected on the year. A volunteer blew the *shofar* to "wake us up" to the new year. All of the children stood on their toes to catch a glimpse of the ram's horn. My daughter stared open-mouthed as she took in the sound. Once the *shofar* had been blasted, it was time to turn my attention to my sins. One by one, I concentrated on each pebble, burning my shortcomings into them as they sat on my sweaty palm. The pebbles didn't mock me. They waited patiently, glinting in the sun, as I thought about what I wanted to change about myself in the coming year. It was weird, from a prayer perspective, that I wasn't asking Jesus to forgive me and help me change. I was going to do it myself with the help of my family and my community. With a deep breath, I cocked my arm back and tossed the pebbles as far as they would go into the water. I watched them plunk and the water ripple in response. A new year. Another year as a Jew. What a gift!

On the day of Yom Kippur, the entire family dressed in white for services. White is both the color used for baptism in Christianity and for atonement each year in Judaism. There are parallels everywhere, which allows Judaism to feel simultaneously familiar and revelatory.

The fact that our year of being Jewish flew by so effortlessly was not lost on me. I really felt like we had settled in and belonged. We were Jewish. I'm not sure when that had sunk in, but it had, seamlessly, at some point after going to the *mikveh* and giving birth to my daughter. We didn't feel as insecure when we failed to recall what a Hebrew phrase meant or when we had to Google how to make cookware kosher.

By the time that Hanukkah rolled around that winter, Travis and I both decided to end our Chicago-Michigan tug of war by taking jobs in New York City. That would mean a third bar exam for me and another move for our young family. But given that New York City had always struck me as the heart of American Jewish life, the decision felt like the right one.

"Are we making the right decision?" Travis asked as he emailed his acceptance to a law firm in Midtown Manhattan.

"Yes," I said firmly. "We'll adjust. We'll make new friends. Our daughter is going to be able to grow up with a huge Jewish community surrounding her. I want that."

"I agree," he said with relief. "I want that, too."

"Good," I smiled, planting a kiss on our daughter's head. We made a nice Jewish family.

CHAPTER 19

"Where there's hope, there's life." *–Anne Frank*

Although the story of our conversion is an ongoing one, I will end in the same place that we began: Christmas. Or Hanukkah. Both.

People often ask if I miss Christianity. This question is difficult to answer. I am a fairly nostalgic person. I miss living in Chicago even though the wind and unreliable public transportation vexed me endlessly while I was there. I sometimes miss my ex-college-flings though I don't think many of them were marriage material. We can miss things while knowing that we don't need to go back to them. They had their time and place.

I sometimes miss the things that I previously associated with Catholicism and Christianity. The smell of incense in a Church, my grandmother's Easter potatoes, and stabbing my finger with an ornament while attempting to decorate a Christmas tree. I don't miss pontificating on my path to heaven or talking incessantly about sin.

As Travis pointed out the day I broached the topic of conversion with him, we live in a Christmas world, and Christmas is the thing that I thought I would miss the most. I am the only person I know who buys eggnog lattes from Starbucks, and my best treadmill performances used to happen with "Joy to the World" playing in the background. I never liked the mess that Christmas trees leave in their wake, but I live for the scent. Hanukkah is not meant to be a replacement for Christmas, but I suppose it's comforting that it takes place around the same time of year. Having a new tradition to swap for the old one eases the feeling of loss as you move from one phase of life to the next.

The first time that I talked to someone about Hanukkah was in college. My sorority had put up a menorah next to the Christmas tree, but I hadn't seen anyone light it or say prayers. The day after the menorah appeared, I had an early morning appointment with the athletic department dietitian. The dietitian's name was Caroline. She had bright blonde hair and a big smile. Her office was flooded with empty oatmeal boxes, cases of Gatorade, and other food items that she had pulled off of the shelves to use in meal-planning conversations. It was the right balance of quirky and professional. Tired and cranky, I trudged to her office in the rain for our scheduled appointment and plopped down into her guest chair with rain-soaked leggings and sopping wet hair.

"Good morning!" she greeted me warmly. "Are you excited for holiday break? It's almost that time." Caroline, of course, knew that I was recovering from an eating disorder, but she didn't make a fuss over it. She stuck to the facts and assured me that her phone line was open any time I wanted to call, day or night.

"I'm not sure about the holidays," I answered. "I'm not ready for everyone to tell me I'm too thin and shove Christmas cookies at me. I'm not really in the cookie spirit this year."

"In fairness," she said lightly, "I don't do Christmas cookies either. But that's because I'm Jewish."

"Oh," I said, perking up at the mention of her Jewishness. "What are you doing for Hanukkah?" The mysterious spark was always there: I needed to know more. Caroline explained that instead of buying her kids gifts, their family bought gifts for *other* kids and donated them. They had recently gathered items to donate for each of the eight nights of Hanukkah and her kids were buzzing with excitement about putting the packages together.

"That's lovely," I told her, "I loved getting gifts when I was a little kid, but eventually you amass so much junk that you can't appreciate it all anymore."

"We prefer to spend time together rather than buying a bunch of new stuff," Caroline explained. "We focus on family, not stuff."

"I'm going to remember that for when I have kids," I told her with a small smile.

And I did remember it. Caroline probably doesn't remember chatting about Hanukkah traditions before coaching me through basic meal planning, but I never forgot. While I enjoyed the give-and-receive nature of

American Christmas celebrations, there was something significantly more heartwarming about doing the giving without doing the taking. The first time that I celebrated Hanukkah, in the weeks before I asked Travis to become Jewish with me, I made a small donation to a different charity every night before lighting our Hanukkah candles. I would continue to do this in subsequent years, and I hope that my daughter will eventually have her own ideas about charities she wants to support. I guess it was our first official Jewish family tradition. Did I swipe it from a college dietitian? Yes. Is that weird? Maybe. Converts have to be creative about how we build our Jewish family lives, so borrowing the traditions of other Jewish families is sometimes part of the process.

Hanukkah is also called the festival of lights. My daughter's Hebrew name, Ora, is the Hebrew word for "light." (It is also the Latin word for "prayer," which I imagine my Protestant great-grandparents had in mind when they named my maternal grandmother). Light is a metaphor for so many things: warmth, truth, levity. Light—to me—has always meant hope. It is the concept of looking for light in the darkness that pulled me through the untimely death of my cousin, my eating disorder, my struggles with the church, and my pregnancy losses. Hanukkah, understated as it is, is a perfect opportunity to remind ourselves that we can be someone else's light in the darkness, and we can also be our own. When we put our menorah in the window during Hanukkah, we remind ourselves that we're called to be a light unto strangers, and when we see someone else's menorah from the street, we're reminded that when we need help, we can allow someone else to be a light unto us. For some people, it is accepting help that feels more unnatural than offering it. Judaism often pushes us to find the balance in these things.

Perhaps it is Hanukkah that I was always longing for. Perhaps that's why I didn't end up missing Christmas as much as I thought I would. Hanukkah was, of course, the first Jewish holiday that I ever really celebrated, about a year before I could properly call myself a Jew. During my first meeting with Liz Berke at Anshe Emet, Travis reiterated his concern that we could never be part of the history that the Jewish people share.

"Well," she said gently, "I think you already are. I think that when you lit those Hanukkah candles and read those ancient prayers, you reached out and claimed a small piece of Jewish history for yourselves. And as you continue to grow and learn in the Jewish tradition, you will be swept up in the course of Jewish history, like Abraham and Sarah and Ruth and all of the other converts before you." I think this conversation is the one that gave my husband the security he needed to take our first steps in the conversion process.

Yom Kippur might be the anniversary of our conversion, but Hanukkah is the anniversary of our commitment to being Jewish. Once my daughter was old enough to point to the candles and smile, it felt even more special. As the baby greased up her face with a latke and stained her shirt with applesauce, Travis sang the Hanukkah prayers in deep, beautiful Hebrew. If someone was watching out their window from the condo across the street, it would appear that we had always been Jewish. I liked it that way. When we lit our candles, it felt like a miracle to be standing there in front of the *hanukkiah* together. Happy, healthy, confident. We made donations to local organizations in order to emphasize to our sweet toddler that it was her responsibility to be the light in the darkness. I still purchased some evergreen tree-scented candles because that smell truly cannot be beat, but I felt at home in Hanukkah like I felt at home in the Jewish people.

Building a Jewish life after conversion doesn't have to be a race. We waited almost three years to do a Jewish wedding ceremony and fill out a *ketubah*, a traditional Jewish marriage contract. I didn't join a Torah study group until I found an amazing one led by Rabbi Danya Ruttenburg—its casual online format let me open up and engage with the text in a way that I was sometimes too shy to do in person. I still haven't memorized the *Shema*, a prayer that I recited every Friday and Saturday at services. I change or alter my Jewish practice every time I move cities and meet new people, exposing me to new Jewish ideas. Everything builds slowly and beautifully.

Potential converts often ask how long it took me to feel a sense of belonging. For me, it ebbs and flows. I felt a little bit Jewish the first time that a woman at Hungarian Kosher Foods asked for my opinion on blintzes, and the time that I was called up for my first *aliyah*. I felt very Jewish when I placed my daughter's tiny hands on the Torah at her baby naming ceremony and when I dressed her up like a spiky pineapple for her first Purim parade.

I felt Jewish when I returned to the *mikveh* for the first time after giving birth, submerging myself again in the warm water, my prayer echoing off the walls of the small chamber. I feel Jewish when I hurl Yiddish insults at unsuspecting motorists on Lakeshore Drive. I felt Jewish when we put together a COVID-era Jewish wedding ceremony and my husband stomped on a glass cup to shouts of "MAZAL TOV."

I feel less Jewish when I admit that I've never tried gefilte fish or when people stumble over my family's French-American surname. I sometimes feel out of place when I hear other Jews read beautifully in Hebrew while I struggle with unfamiliar words. We still grapple with how to build our own Jewish practice from scratch. We struggle to figure out what we think about important Jewish issues like *tznius* (modesty), fasting, or how to interpret certain Torah portions. We also struggle with small issues like how we feel about months-long Jewish summer camps, superstition, or how much one should spend on Judaica.

When other Jews talk about their incredible family history and immigration patterns, I typically sit silently. When rabbis refer to "our ancestors," it sometimes strikes me that they are only mine in spirit. Mostly, though, I recognize that it's incumbent upon me to build Jewish history with my family today even if I can't change the fact that my family's ancestry and the ancestry of the Jewish people is not one and the same.

Back when I was in Berlin with the FASPE program and not yet Jewish, I came upon a photo of a post-war refugee camp for Jews. One particular photo stuck with me over all of the months and years since I took that trip. There were five or six Jewish children crowded around an older gentleman at a simple table with a scrap of white tablecloth draped over it. There is a braided loaf of challah on the table. The adult in the photo is looking at the camera, the ghost of a smile playing across his features. The children are thin and their faces smudged with dirt, but some of them are smirking in the way that happy, mischievous children do. They look tired and a bit sad, as if they've been through hell. Indeed, they had been. But standing around that table on what I can only imagine was a Friday night, they are the picture of hope and resilience. In their eyes, there is light. I cannot hope to understand what they and their ancestors have been through. I can only marvel that the same force that sustained their faith during some of the darkest days of human history is the same mysterious, otherworldly force that guided me to a Jewish life. *Baruch Hashem.*

AFTER

When Ora was about a year old, our small family was invited to a children's Passover seder at a kosher restaurant on Wall Street. An Orthodox rabbi had seen our family taking a mid-morning Shabbos walk and immediately identified us as fellow Jews. He shouted "good Shabbos" from across the street and made his way over to Ora's stroller to strike up a conversation. Travis wasn't wearing a *kippah* that day, so we never reached an agreement on how the rabbi had picked us out. Maybe he had guessed; more likely, he shouts "good Shabbos" at everyone and hopes for a promising response. In any case, we were delighted. The rabbi engaged us in a brief conversation and urged us to bring Ora to the seder to meet the other Jewish kids in the neighborhood. We accepted the invitation.

"You two really know Jewish law," he said before we parted ways, "Did you go to Yeshiva as teenagers?" Travis and I smiled conspiratorially and told him that we did not.

The seder was held on the rooftop of the restaurant under a clear sky in late March. Sleepy from the previous night's seder, we carried our daughter up the narrow staircase and plopped her down in a chair next to a plastic seder plate and a bottle of Kedem grape juice. I smoothed my long black-and-white holiday dress and looked around. To our right was New York Harbor, shining in the late afternoon light. In front of us were the tall buildings of the Financial District, reaching toward the sky and obscuring our view of the rest of Manhattan.

"I can't believe we live in New York. And we're Jewish," I told Travis as Ora made a beeline for the other kids in search of a playmate.

"Should we tell him we converted?" Travis asked.

"I can't see why it would matter at this juncture," I shrugged. He agreed.

It was hard to imagine a more perfect evening. The weather was gorgeous, and Ora was wearing her most adorable holiday skirt with a tiny black-and-white blazer. The rabbi's daughter put on a private puppet show with a matzoh plush toy for Ora, who giggled delightedly while chasing her new curly-haired friend around the rooftop.

When all of the families had arrived and gotten settled, the rabbi's wife led all of us through an abbreviated seder. When it came time for the children to sing "Ma Nishtana," my daughter clapped along on beat while I stumbled over some of the Hebrew. Ora had clearly practiced the song at her Jewish daycare and was easily outshining me. After singing and cramming her face with boiled eggs and potatoes dipped in saltwater, my daughter eyed the kosher-for-Passover rainbow cake with burning desire. Her blazer was studded with bits of crumbling egg yolk, and she was high on grape juice and childish delight.

SHANNON GONYOU

"Just a small piece, sweetie," I said, offering her the paper plate filled with flourless Passover cakes and cookies. Grinning broadly, Ora snatched both a cookie and a piece of cake and then escaped from her chair and bolted away from us. By the time I caught up with her, she was running circles around the rabbi, spitting bits of red and green cake at his black dress shoes.

"I think that's enough sugar," Travis chuckled nervously, apologizing to the rabbi for the mess on the floor.

"But it's Pesach!" he exclaimed, throwing his arms wide and smiling.

"Yes," I said, "I think this might be her new favorite holiday." Ora was now working on her second dessert and affectionately squeezing a rubber frog that the rabbi's wife had brought for the Ten Plagues story.

"I don't think that frog belongs to her," I told Travis. "Sorry," I said sheepishly to the rabbi, trying to extricate the frog from Ora's slimy fingers.

"You know what?" the rabbi boomed, "She can have another frog. And another piece of cake. Let. Them. Enjoy it! Let them take delight in their holidays. Let them make wonderful memories. Let them grow up and remember eating so much rainbow cake that they couldn't eat anymore. That's what we're here for: the joy. Without that, there's no point."

I looked over my shoulder at the sun setting over Manhattan, and at the children dancing around in their Pesach outfits, covered in grape juice and saltwater and bits of horseradish. Some of them would grow up to take the Passover story literally, others as metaphor. Some would keep strictly kosher for Passover, others would not. Some would host traditional seders in the future, others would host seders based on social justice or feminism. The world of Judaism was wide open to them because it belonged to them, too. I was so very proud to pass this tradition down to my daughter.

It is so very joyful to be Jewish.